SPIRITUAL AWAKENINGS
Illuminations on Shabbat
and the Holidays

Spiritual Awakenings
Illuminations on Shabbat and the Holidays

YEHOSHUA RUBIN

edited by Shoshana Lepon

URIM PUBLICATIONS

New York • Jerusalem

Spiritual Awakenings:
Illuminations on Shabbat and the Holidays
by Yehoshua Rubin
edited by Shoshana Lepon
Copyright © 2003 by Yehoshua Rubin

First Edition. Printed at Hemed Press, Israel.

ISBN 965-7108-41-1

Urim Publications, P.O.BOX 52287, Jerusalem 91521 Israel

Lambda Publishers Inc.
3709 13th Avenue Brooklyn, New York 11218 U.S.A.
Tel: 718-972-5449 Fax: 718-972-6307
Email: mh@ejudaica.com

www.UrimPublications.com

Designed by Raphaël Freeman
Typeset in Garamond by Jerusalem Typesetting

Contents

Contents

My Own Spiritual Awakening

1 HAVE NO PROBLEM waking up — as long as it's after 9:00 A.M. Before that, I have a deep aversion to getting out of bed. In fact, none of my family are early risers, and my wife Annette would pay any amount of money to be able to huddle under the covers all morning, which is pretty hard to do in this Middle Eastern climate.

In Israel, Sunday is just another day of work and school. And so, with much effort, Annette, myself and our four children are bundled out of the house by 7:30. At that hour, we are not much to look at. We're awake, but as we go through the motions of putting one foot in front of the other, we're still pretty much asleep. It's what I call "awake-sleep-walking."

Awake-sleep-walking is pretty much a parable for my life. Over the years, much of my time has been occupied with awake-sleep-walking. I was awake and doing my thing in this world: getting degrees, teaching, making money, having children…but all the while, I felt that I was asleep.

You know, I kind of liked my awake-sleep-walking existence. When I was awake-asleep, I did what I was supposed to do, didn't get in trouble and escaped as often as possible into the dreamlike world of TV and movies (mostly Star Trek — the original series).

You want to know why I awake-sleep-walked? Awake-sleep-walking allowed me to acquire what society expected me to have:

- A house
- A car
- Life insurance
- A healthy bank account
- A BA; an MA; rabbinical ordination
- A wife and kids.

I never asked myself: Is this what I really want? Is this what I need? There is another reason I chose to awake-sleep-walk. It enabled me to avoid dealing with the pain I felt inside: the pain of the young child being held in low regard; the troubled teenage panic of losing control over my life; and, as an adult, the searing heartache of rejection from women I wanted to call my own.

Yet by age 28, I was ready to ask myself: What is life all about? Why do I need what I have? Why do I have all this pain and what am I supposed to do with it? It was at this point in my life that I turned to the traditional Jewish sources. Through extensive study, long talks with rabbis, and much soul-searching with friends, I found the following answer: Life is about waking up. It's about engaging in real life with all its disappointments and successes. It's about allowing ourselves to feel both the pain and the ecstasy of life.

Once I figured that out, I no longer wanted to be an awake-sleep-walker. I wanted to feel every moment. I wanted to be awake every single moment. It was then that I began to spend more time with myself – my entire self – even with pain. I began to spend much more time with my family and tried to make this time sweet. The result was that my life became more meaningful and significant.

Luckily for me, I found that Shabbat and the Jewish holidays were a guide to the spiritual awakenings that I needed in order to wake up and stay awake. Through celebrating these special days I discovered what life is about: Tasting the sweetness of this world. Feeling the love your spouse has for you. Tickling your children. Learning to take advantage of Shabbat's gift of rest. Learning to forgive and give second chances on Yom Kippur. Experiencing the Tu B'Shvat process of turning dreams into realities, as a seed turns itself into a fruit-bearing tree. Being a Purim Jew when you let down your barriers and fall in love with every human being. Learning to transform your pain into empathy as you leave your own personal Egypt at your Passover *seder*. And it's about staying up all night on Shavuot, to become as spiritually awakened as Ruth, the Moabite, when she opened up her eyes.

Friends, this book is a map to the hidden treasure I found. I share it with you so that you can know just how beautiful, sweet, meaningful and joyous your Judaism can be. It is my hope that after reading this book, you'll want to spend more time with those you love. It is my hope that you'll feel spiritually richer, spiritually awakened, and that you'll write to share your "spiritual awakenings" with me.

Love and blessings,
Yehoshua Rubin

Thank you...

To God, for giving the Jewish people all these wonderful and special days.

To my mother, Judy Rubin, for showing how much happiness and meaning these days can bring to our lives.

To my father, Rabbi Yitzchak Rubin, who taught me from the youngest age the deepest philosophical understanding of these special days. His ideas live on through my writing.

To my grandfather, Rabbi Phillip Goodman, for being such a writer's role model. Saba, this is book number one. I hope to reach your achievement of thirteen volumes.

To Rabbi Aaron Rakeffet, who taught me "Passionate Judaism."

To Rabbi Shlomo Riskin, who showed me the light in Jewish Law.

To Rabbi Aryeh Ben David, who helped me develop as a teacher at Livnot U'Lehibanot, where I was able to cultivate many of the ideas found in this book.

To Livnot, for including many of my articles in their weekly Internet magazine at www.livnot.org.il.

To Michael Even Aish, my Livnot editor, who always encouraged me.

To Rabbi Shlomo Carlebach, may his memory be for a blessing, who showed me that Judaism is an infinite present, which we can only open if we, as well, strive towards infinity.

To my neighbor, Sara Shendelson, for being so patient and listening to all my rewrites. Her many contributions helped me make this work my very best.

To Shoshana Lepon, for taking the individual notes of this manuscript and transforming them into the sweetest symphony.

Thank you to all those who kept me spiritually awake:

Rabbi David Aaron, Sara Ben David, Rabbi Shmuel Bowman, Charlie Buckholtz, Yafit Clymer, Rabbi David Ebner, Rabbi Mimi Feigelson, Rabbi David Fink, Dr. Aryeh Geiger, Mordechai Goldberg, Rabbi Gedalyah Gurfein, Rick Himmelman, Rabbi Shlomo Kimchi, David Kronish, Daniel and Bryna Levy, Dr. Avraham Moskowitz, Omer Nurik, Rut Yair-Nussbaum, Tovya and Mike Paris, Rabbi Meir and Gila Rosen, Rabbi Menachem Schraeder, Rabbi Meir Shweiger, Rabbi Natan Siegel, Mick Weinstein, Shaya ben Yehuda, and Rabbi David and Sara Zeller.

To my children, for bringing so much life, joy and happiness to our Shabbatot and holidays.

And, finally, to my wife, Annette. I thank you for all your love, encouragement and direction. It is your presence and mindfulness that has transformed our Shabbatot and holidays into Holy Days.

Shabbat

A Time to Press Pause

Six days shall you spend time with the world
And on the seventh shall you spend time with yourself
and your dear ones

$\mathcal{A}$ TYPICAL DAY in our lives: Get up at 6:00 A.M. Get kids off to school. Commute to work. Make heroic efforts not to lose my temper when students act up in school. Mark papers. Deal with complaining parents. Work till 3:00 P.M., commute back. Buy fresh bread and milk on the way home, throw in a load of laundry, and sit down to lunch with my four children.... Ketchup! Get up to bring the ketchup. Watch the kids squeeze ketchup on the food, on their faces, on their clothing.... Homework! Take old, moldy sandwiches out of school bags, sharpen pencils, and make sure their books and notebooks are ready for the next day. Activities! Pasting, coloring, reading books. Move the clothing from washer to dryer. Make dinner and coffee, extra caffeine, extra sugar. Sweep, set the table for supper. More ketchup! More on the food, more on their faces, more on their clothing.... By now, we are exhausted. If we can just get through supper and get them to bed, we'll be free.

Free time for us! YEAH!

Dinner is almost over when I look up and see the sun setting. So beautiful, I think to myself. What a great moment to share with the kids – if only I had the strength. I'm just twenty minutes away from putting my feet up and vegging-out in front of the video. If I take them outside, it means 10 minutes to get shoes and coats on, 15 minutes to enjoy the sunset and another 20 minutes to get them back home and into bed.

I struggle with the decision.

Finally I turn to my kids and say, "Everybody get your coats on and grab a blanket! We are going outside to watch the sunset."

After much huffing and puffing, we all trundle out to the back of the house. The sun is setting, the stars begin to emerge, and there's a cool breeze as we snuggle under our blankets.

Suddenly, Shayna turns to me and says, "Daddy, I love you."

Shayna had something very important to share with me at that moment. She had her love. But in order to share it, she needed the time and the setting.

I could have missed hearing those words from my daughter.

I could have missed the sunset.

I could have missed the cool breeze and the snuggling under blankets.

But I stopped and made the time.

This is one of the fundamental purposes of Shabbat. Shabbat exists so we won't miss the sunsets or the breezes or the snuggles of our lives. Shabbat exists so we can take the time to sit.

The word Shabbat actually means, "to sit," and this day is about learning to do just that. Sit and listen. Sit and don't miss your life passing by.

Sit and hear it.

Create a time when all you have to do is look at God's creation. If you look long enough it begins to speak to you. But it can't speak unless you give it the time and the setting. It can't speak unless you listen.

Sit.

Create a time that does not compete with the TV. It's just you and the ones you feel closest to.

Sit and enjoy their company.

Sit. Talk with them. Have you spent more time today with your computer or with your friends?

Sit. Mellow out and let them share something special with you. They, too, need the proper atmosphere: the sunset, the cool breeze, the snuggle, and, mostly, the time.

Sitting on Shabbat gives us the strength to reenter the weekday world more attuned to where we want to be, what we want to experience, and what we want to make sure not to miss. Shabbat offers the gift of time. This is why the laws of Shabbat call for turning off the outside world. We keep away from radio, e-mail and telephones. We refrain from doing business, writing, painting, shopping and planting.

During the week we are so busy. Why?

Often, the reason for this business of "busyness" is so that we don't have to think about where we are or where we're going. It's easier just to continue on our way. What if I think about where I am and realize that there are no sunsets or snuggles in my life? What if I think about my future and find that the sun is only setting and not rising? We create noise to drown out the voice we need to hear the most – our very own.

Yet, deep inside of all of us is a spiritual desire to be still and bring up what's hidden within our hearts. Deep inside, we desire to have a day of rest, a day set aside for writing on our insides, painting our souls and planting our own ideas. The peace of Shabbat allows the soul the space it needs to sprout roots and grow.

In the West we are taught how to run. In the East we are taught how to sit. In Judaism we strike a balance.

Six days shall you run and on the seventh shall you sit.

Six days shall you spend time with the world and on the seventh shall you spend time with yourself and your dear ones. There are so many sunsets, so many "I love you's," so many deep spiritual moments to experience. So once every seven days we go through a process that has been repeated week after week, year after year, since the beginning of time. We enter into Shabbat and welcome the quiet. The quiet that allowed Shayna's soul to burst open and say, "Daddy, I love you."

The quiet of Shabbat allows our soul to find its voice.

On Friday night at sundown, we welcome Shabbat with the lighting of candles – symbolic of our own internal light. The rising, dancing flames of the candles mirror our soul's urge to connect to its Divine source.

We sit with family and guests around a table laden with traditional Shabbat food, and we sing. We sing songs about universal peace and songs about a more perfect world. We sing songs of appreciation for the sustenance God provides us with, and we awaken our inner selves through our song.

We share words of Torah at the Shabbat table, refocusing our goals by discussing the issues presented in the weekly portion.

Shabbat is a taste of everything we don't want to miss in life. It's a day of spiritual awakening.

What is the goal? The goal is to snuggle. Not once a year, once a month, or even once a week on Shabbat. The goal is to achieve a daily snuggle and a daily sunset and a daily "I love you."

The goal is to take Shabbat with us into the week.

We wait for the day when everyone in the world can join in our Shabbat peace. On the day of the eternal Sabbath, there will be true rest for the spirit and true succor for the soul.

Shabbat Shalom!

Learning to Let Go

Six days shall you hold on tight
and on the seventh day shall you let go

No one likes to be told, "Don't do this" and "Don't do that." So when Judaism comes out with a long, detailed shopping list of acts that are prohibited on Shabbat, our knee-jerk reaction is to cry foul. What about our freedom of choice?

Ah, freedom. We need to understand that choosing to refrain from certain actions on Shabbat is a special freedom granted to us. We are free to let go. We are free to relinquish control and we are free to rest. By following the Divine "manufacturer's directions," we gain an important spiritual awakening.

When we allow ourselves a day of rest, it follows that we allow God's entire world a day of rest. We don't plow to prepare the land for planting. We don't water plants or mow the lawn. We don't light or extinguish fires, even a tiny spark of electricity.

The goal is to loosen our grip over the physical world.

However, this raises a question: God gave humankind the job of working and perfecting the world. "Rule the world and subdue it..." was the biblical commandment given to Adam and Eve. We can only fix the world by learning how to harness and make use of the forces of nature. It is through our efforts to control the physical world that we now live in such a state of technological advancement. So why stop all this progress for Shabbat?

Because letting go is a very important part of life. In a relationship, you can only get to know your partner by letting go; only then will you be able to really understand him or her. This is true in any relationship because when you relinquish control, you are ultimately giving the other person a chance to come to the surface. If you are determined always to be on top, you'll never hear what the other person has to say.

Letting go of the land, the animals, other people, and especially ourselves, is a reminder that everything has the right to exist for its own sake. The practice of relinquishing control once a week balances out the side of us that needs to master everything around us for our own benefit.

In Deuteronomy 5:12 it says:

> Guard the Sabbath to keep it holy.... Six days shall you labor and do all your work; but the seventh day is Sabbath to the Lord, your God; you shall not do any work – you, your son, your daughter...your animals and the foreigner who is within your gates. Your male and female slaves shall rest just as you do. And you shall remember that you were slaves in Egypt, and the Lord, your God, brought you out.... It is for this reason that the Lord, your God, has commanded you to keep the Sabbath.

This passage reveals that within each of us there is an enslaving Pharaoh. The Pharaohs were rulers who operated by controlling all those around them. They built the Great Pyramids of Egypt with slave labor, and decreed that their wives and servants be buried alive with them when they died. The Pharaohs lived in the fifteenth century B.C.E., yet every time we become impatient with the person behind the check-out counter, the waiter or the taxi driver, we are giving voice to Pharaoh's words: I control you now.

When we live in this manner, seeking our own personal benefit without considering the wider ramifications of our actions, the internal

Pharaoh begins to rule our lives. Along comes Shabbat to teach that for six days we are active in the world, but for one day a week we become its liberator.

Six days paint; on the seventh day stand back and admire.

Six days cook and bake; on the seventh day stop to taste God's bounty.

Six days do your business dealings; on the seventh day enjoy some peace.

Six days raise your children; on the seventh day sit down with them and sing.

Six days hold on tight; on the seventh day let go.

We make the world a better place by freeing everyone and everything on Shabbat.

Learning To Be At Peace With Yourself

It is not good for man to be alone

(Genesis 2:25)

*W*E LIVE IN A CULTURE based on control, and that control can be hazardous to our health. Take, for example, pill popping. Why do we take so much medication? Because we want to have as much control as possible over our physical discomforts.

If we were to let go, we would first reach for a chair, breathe deeply and try to relax, allowing the pain to surface. This would help us learn more about our body and what it's trying to tell us.

If we would keep away from the medicine chest and its "quick fix" formulas, we might begin to wake up to our problems and identify the root of our discomfort. Perhaps this headache comes from unacknowledged stress, from an unbalanced diet, from lack of sleep or from the fact that it's been so long since we've taken the time to play.

In Judaism we're taught, "It is not good for man to be alone" (Genesis 2:25). We are born alone, and this loneliness creates a painful sense of emptiness. We spend our entire lives trying to deal with it, one way or another. Letting go means turning off the TV, taking off the Walkman, putting down the mystery novel, hanging up the phone, and just listening to the quiet around us. Letting go means learning to be empty. It means learning to feel the pain, because only by allowing that pain to surface can we begin to address it and fill its needs.

Ask yourselves this: What do I really need in order not to feel lonely anymore? How long will I use Jay Leno as an adult-size baby bottle to pacify myself to sleep? How long will I stay in this relationship just so I won't be left by myself? How many sessions with the psychologist am I going to pay for just to hear him say that life means being lonely at times?

Only when we learn to let go and hear the voice of our emptiness can we learn from it. Why am I empty? What do I really need to fill my emptiness? What did people do before there was TV? Do you think they sat in their living rooms staring at the wall, saying, "Boy, I can't wait till someone invents the TV?"

Judaism teaches that we're all born incomplete. There is no way out. We must accept our human reality and revel in our strengths and weaknesses, because that's who we are. Shabbat is a day to be yourself, your true self. If you feel full – great! If you feel empty – that's fine, too. Shabbat is a day to wake up and go with the flow, the flow of the universe, without trying to fight and control it.

Candlelighting:
Igniting the Inner Flame

A mitzvah is a candle and Torah is light
(Proverbs 6:23)

"MOMMY! DADDY! At Jessica's house they light Shabbat candles. How come we don't?" You look down at your little girl and you know an intellectual response won't answer her question. You also know it won't silence the emotional turmoil this question creates inside of you.

Did my mother light Shabbat candles? Did my grandmother? Did my great-grandmother? Who knows? But for sure my great-great grandmother lit Shabbat candles, although she probably called it "*licht bentching*." For thousands of years, our grandparents illuminated Jewish history with their flickering Sabbath lights.

Our grandmothers saw that all of us have a candle in our soul, so they decided to light one Shabbat candle for each member of the family. These women were responsible for the institution of this law, and subsequently passed on the tradition.

When we light candles on Friday afternoon, we create a grandmother standing beside us, pointing right at our hearts. And that grandmother, that *Bubby*, is saying: Take the light inside yourself. Let it illuminate the way to your internal light.

"Which candle is mine?" is the weekly refrain in our house. My

27

children always want to know where they stand in this proud procession of flickering flames. Can there be a greater gift than the gift of light? Once a week we begin a spiritual day with a spiritual message. There is light in the world – a light that exists inside of all of us. Shabbat is a day to be at one with our internal light. We can have a spiritual awakening by asking such questions as: How do I light up my life, my family, my world? How would I like to bring out more light?

King Solomon says in Proverbs, "A *mitzvah* is a candle and Torah is light."

King Solomon knew that the Hebrew word *mitzvah* – commandment – comes from the same root as the words *tzavta* and *tzevet* which connote "connectedness." A candle is a connection because we feel connected to God, to ourselves and to others when we gaze at its light. When we light Shabbat candles we are trying to connect to a deeper light. How do we know when we have really learned to do this? How do we know when we have gained a spiritual awakening? When the light warms our heart to such a degree that we feel connected to the people standing beside us as we kindle the flame.

At that moment, we feel connected not only to our grandmothers, but to our spouses, our children, our friends and, most important, to ourselves.

Kabbalat Shabbat: Dancing Through Life

Hitoreree, hitoreree – Awaken, awaken!

REB AARON of Karlin was asked: "Why do your *chassidim* dance during the Friday night service?" Gazing at his disciples who were spinning round and round, he answered, "Because when they dance, they begin to raise themselves up off the ground."

When we dance, one foot is rooted in the physical world while the other reaches towards heaven. This kind of dancing characterizes the Friday night prayer service, which we begin by praising God for the physical world, for the hidden mysteries of nature – the trees with their marvelous shapes and colors, the rivers and oceans that carry water from all parts of the world with tremendous force, and the mountains that try so desperately to reach the skies above.

When we contemplate the world around us, we are spiritually awakened by its beauty and grandeur. This leads us to turn in awe and gratitude to the One who created it all. The Friday night service includes six psalms which correspond to the six days of the week. These psalms are meant to help us reconnect to the physical world with a deeper spiritual perspective. The climax of these psalms is a poem called *Lecha*

Dodi. Even those congregations that rush through the first six psalms cannot help bursting out in song when they reach *Lecha Dodi.*

Lecha Dodi means, "Come, my Beloved." We sing to welcome the Shabbat Queen into our world. Shabbat is the dream of a perfect world for which the Jewish people have been praying for thousands of years. As we sing *Lecha Dodi,* we say, *Hitna'ari me'afar kumi* – "Shake yourself off and rise from the dust," and *Hitoreree, hitoreree,* which calls for us to "Awaken, awaken!" The time for a more perfect world is at hand.

To be Jewish is to hold onto a dream, a special dream – a spiritual dream of the future. Yet if we really want it to happen, holding on is not enough. We must sing our dream and even dance our dream. Through our singing and dancing, we breathe new life into our physical existence and reconnect to the promise of the future.

Although in this world we have no choice but to remain with one foot planted on the earth, we must still dance the dance of Reb Aaron's *chassidim.* We must lift our other foot and reach for the heavens. And we must teach our children this dance step, too.

As we dance, one foot is rooted in the present while the other is yearning for the Shabbat to come. You don't have to be a *chassid* to know the secret of dancing through life. You just have to catch the Shabbat melody and do the steps.

Shabbat Shalom:
Breaking Through Barriers

Be sure to greet every person with a pleasant countenance
(Ethics of the Fathers 1:15)

*W*E CAN HARDLY WAIT: every Friday night, when we leave the synagogue, a miracle occurs. Everyone turns and blesses each other with a blessing of peace, *Shabbat Shalom* – "Good Shabbos." Then an even greater miracle happens. As we walk down the street, we bless everyone we see, "Good Shabbos!"

Miracle, you say, what miracle? Greeting people on the street is not a miracle. A miracle is God splitting the Red Sea! But think about it.... How hard do you think it was for the Almighty to split a body of water? And how much strength do we need, as mortal human beings, to break through the invisible walls that separate us?

We live in a world where we avoid other people's eyes. We walk with our face to the ground, or our head held high. We put on make-believe blinders and pass people by, not showing any form of recognition. We get so caught up in our own reality that we lose sight of the world around us. We forget that there are people in this world who survive on the simple acts of sharing that we take for granted.

Rabbi Shlomo Carlebach taught, in the name of Reb Nachman of Breslov, that when people walk into a room and we ignore them, we are basically killing them. When we ignore someone, we send a message: For me, you do not exist. We forget that a lack of communication speaks louder than any spoken message.

The Shabbat world is one in which barriers fall, a world in which we find the spiritual strength to tear down walls. We awaken to the holiness inherent in this day, giving us the strength to greet everyone we see and bless them.

When the Messiah comes, we will value the uniqueness of every human being. We can hardly wait; we must start now by learning how to say, "*Shalom.*"

Shabbat Shalom.

Shalom Aleichem: Bringing it Home

Peace be unto you, Angels of Peace
(from the *Shalom Aleichem* prayer)

WE HAVE ENTERED the spiritual essence of Shabbat through our prayer in synagogue and our greetings to others on the street. We feel so elevated. Now we enter our home, where the most difficult and satisfying challenge awaits us – the challenge of bringing home our dream of peace.

We start the Shabbat evening meal with the song *Shalom Aleichem* – "Peace be unto you." *Shalom Aleichem Malachei HaSharet* – We welcome the "Angels of Peace" into our homes, into our families.

Shalom Aleichem. We are praying to God to please, please grant heavenly peace amongst warring nations. But how can we have peace between nations when we don't even have peace among the members of our family? When we sing *Shalom Aleichem*, we are praying: Please, please, we need so much peace in this house. Peace between husband and wife. Peace between parents and children. Peace between brother and sister....

Whom can we hurt the most? Those who are closest to us. I am so close to you, my partner, my children, my parents. Why do I cause you so much pain?

33

Shalom Aleichem. We must learn to sing it together. And we must yearn for a different reality. An angelic one, where instead of hurting those closest to me, I am able to strengthen them and lift them up.

Shalom Aleichem means "Peace be unto you." It means learning how to give peace to someone else. Rabbi Shlomo Carlebach taught that everyone wants to *have* peace; the question is how many people are willing to *give* it?

Eshet Chayil: Making Room

Who will find a woman of valor?

(Proverbs 31:10)

*A*T SOME POINT we all grow out of our teenage romantic fantasies and begin to think about what is important to search for in a partner. On Friday night, as we sing *Eshet Chayil*, we enumerate these qualities. *Eshet Chayil* means "a woman of valor." Why was woman chosen to symbolize all the qualities that are praiseworthy in a relationship?

Judaism recognizes two kinds of strengths: the male strength to build walls, and the female strength to tear them down. At times, we need to insulate ourselves from the world around us, so we build walls between ourselves and others. There are many who would harm us or take advantage of us if we were totally open with them. These people would invade our privacy and trample our feelings.

The male strength of building walls explains the subway phenomenon. Why do subways seem so crowded? Because each car is filled, not just with people, but also with all the walls that shield them from each other. Imagine if the same number of people got into the same subway car, but they were all good friends. There would be so much more room!

Building these barriers, for better or for worse, is considered a male strength. But there is another type of strength, and that is relationship

35

strength. It is the strength to break the ice, break down walls and make room for one another. This is the strength described in *Eshet Chayil*.

We sing: *Batach bah lev ba'alah* – "Her husband's heart is safe with her." *Vatakom be'od lailah* – "And she arises while it is still night [to give food to her family]." *Kapah parsah le'ani* – "Her palm is open to the poor." *Torat chesed al leshonah* – "The philosophy of loving kindness is on her lips."

In a world where more relationships fall apart than stay together, the *Eshet Chayil* knows that the glue is made up of giving. When do relationships begin to disintegrate? When we take more than we give.

Both Kabbalah and child psychology explain the power of the woman. Kabbalah teaches that physical realities reflect spiritual realities; a similiar idea is found in the writings of child psychologist, Erik Erikson, who wrote that "Anatomy is destiny."

A woman's biological makeup teaches the spiritual lesson of making room inside oneself for another. Just as her ability to make room for the baby is that which allows the parent-child relationship to form, so, too, all relationships begin when we learn to make room for the other.

There are those who view relationships as a form of confinement. I have to take other people's likes and dislikes into account, thereby limiting my own choices. I have to do things I would rather not do, such as going shopping or doing the dishes. Yet a woman's physical/spiritual reality teaches that constriction is expansion. As I learn to limit myself and make way for others, I am actually expanding. I am able to bring new life into the world.

As we sing *Eshet Chayil*, we are singing of the strengths needed to create lasting commitments. We are singing about the very basis of a perfect world.

As we sing this song, we should be ready for a uniquely feminine spiritual awakening. We should look for relationship strengths within ourselves and within our spouses or partners-to-be, for these strengths will take us one step closer to the day that is totally Shabbat, the Messianic day when the world will be one.

Blessing Our Children:
Finding a Spiritual Home

You can only raise your children
if you learn how to raise yourself
(Rabbi Abraham J. Twerski)

*F*RIDAY NIGHT, at the Shabbat table, is a time for a parent to bestow the threefold biblical blessing found in Numbers 6:24–26, as well as a private blessing.

May God bless and guard you – a blessing for physical well-being.

May God's light shine on you and educate you – a blessing for emotional and intellectual growth.

May God turn toward you and give you peace – a blessing for balance between all our human drives. Perfect balance is the Jewish perception of peace.

As we bless our children, we convey two very important messages. With the biblical blessing, I am leading my children along an ancient spiritual path. I am telling them that there is much to treasure in the wisdom of old. Secondly, by performing the act of blessing, I am showing my children that I, myself, as their parent, am a source of strength and blessing.

For me, the weekly custom of blessing my children on Friday

night before eating the Shabbat meal started me on the path to finding a spiritual home. Facing my children forced me to face my strengths and weaknesses. For a long time it was difficult for me to stand and bless them, because I would hesitate, remembering all the mistakes I had made during the week.

I realized, with time and the help of my wife, that this moment was a golden opportunity. I could use it to recognize my weaknesses and try to fix them. This Shabbat custom became a weekly opportunity to focus on my children. A time to awaken spiritually as a parent and ask myself:

- How do I connect with my children?
- Do I have something of substance to give them?
- Do I have the strength to help them answer their question: Why am I here?

This ritual became the weekly climax of my job as a parent. It felt so good to be in a process of growth. I finally understood Rabbi Twerski's words: "You can only raise your children if you learn how to raise yourself."

Parenting is a tool for spiritual growth because it forces us to reach deep inside ourselves and find our personal core. Blessing my children forces me to ponder what I want to give over to them and what I want them to take from me as they walk through this life. For this reason, there are those who say that parenting begins ten years before our children are born.

The act of blessing our children reinforces our love for them, making them feel at home. We are, at the same time, making them feel at home within their heritage. Finding a place called home is such a special thing. And once we have found it, we should try to visit at least once a week. In Judaism we pay a visit home regularly – every single Shabbat.

Kiddush:
Getting High on Spirituality

For it is the first of all the days of holiness,
in commemoration of the Exodus from Egypt
(from *Kiddush*)

*A*T THE SHABBAT TABLE we lift a cup filled with wine as we recite *Kiddush*. Lifting the cup during *Kiddush* signifies spiritual elevation. Usually people drink because they want to get high. Indeed, we should spend our whole life getting high. The question is: What gets you high? As we recite *Kiddush*, we are singing about those things that get us high in a Jewish way.

Kiddush consists of two paragraphs, with the blessing for wine sandwiched in the middle. The first paragraph describes how God created the seventh day as a day of spiritual awakenings.

- A day to encounter our higher selves.
- A day to experience nature, not as a taker but as an admirer.
- A day to focus on our heritage.
- A day to strengthen ties with family and friends.

In Judaism, we believe it is these encounters – with our world, our heritage, ourselves and our loved ones – that create a spiritual high. It's the failure to cope with these encounters that brings so many of us down.

The second paragraph of *Kiddush* deals with the spiritual elevation of the Jewish people. The Jewish people are entrusted with a sacred mission – a mission that needed us to start off as slaves in Egypt, so that we would eternally carry with us a loathing of slavery.

Kiddush speaks of the Jews as the chosen nation – chosen to remember the Exodus – chosen to remind ourselves and everyone else that no one has the right to enslave another. There is nothing that gets you higher than freedom, true freedom – as opposed to enslavement to drugs, alcohol, social pressures and the media (the media is not interested in me being me, but in me being whatever they are advertising).

In Judaism, freedom begins when we see the uniqueness in ourselves and in others. We use wine for *Kiddush* because we are making a toast to physical and spiritual freedom.

Wine comes from pressing grapes. Rabbi Shlomo Carlebach taught that this is symbolic of our world. Many times we succeed in this world by stepping on others, like people stomping on grapes. Yet Shabbat shows us a perfect world. In a perfect world, we can get ahead in life without stepping on others. We take that which was created through being stepped on and lift it up high. And we learn that nothing gets you higher than lifting up someone else.

Lifting Our Hands and Eating the Bread

Lift up your hands in holiness and bless God

(Psalms 134:2)

*F*OLLOWING *Kiddush*, we perform two acts which teach the lesson of spiritual elevation: washing our hands and eating the bread.

Jewish Law prescribes the washing of our hands before we eat bread. This must be done in a very specific manner: The washing cup is picked up with the right hand and passed over to the left. The left hand pours over the right hand, then the right hand takes the cup and pours over the left. This is done twice; a blessing is then said. As in many aspects of Judaism, the details seem bothersome and ritualistic. If I picked up the cup with my left hand instead of my right, what would it matter?

Another issue is the wording of the blessing: "Blessed are you, God, Master of the Universe, who has commanded us to lift our hands." Why do we refer to lifting instead of washing?

The answer to both these questions is found in the Kabbalah. According to the *Zohar*, our left side represents our need to judge while our right side represents our need to be compassionate. The cup is passed and poured in this way because in life there are some times when we need more judgment, and there are other times when more compassion is called for. One pours onto the other.

However, this ritual washing begins with the right hand – compassion – and ends with compassion being poured over judgment: right over left. The wording of the blessing is now clear. By doing this exercise in "lifting our hands" and elevating our lives, we are learning how to be more compassionate than judgmental.

This gives new meaning to the phrase, "My hands are clean." This usually means, "I didn't do it." However, with this type of washing, I *did* do something. My hands are clean, not because I avoided taking action, but because I did an exercise in acting positively.

It is also customary to actually lift up our hands after pouring the water and look at them. By looking at our hands, we become cognizant of their actions. It is our hands that allow us to write, paint, play music, sew, build, and stroke our loved ones. It is our hands that express human creativity. As we lift and gaze at this wonderful gift, we must make an honest appraisal of how we have used them.

The second act of spiritual elevation is the blessing we say over the *challah*, our special Shabbat bread. My father, Rabbi Yitzchak Rubin, always brought our attention to the wording: "Blessed are you, God, Master of the Universe, who brings bread from the earth."

I can still hear my father's voice, passionate with conviction, as he explained, "We all know that bread does not come from the earth. Wheat, yes; bread, no. Yet the wording is no mistake. Bread is the Jewish symbol of food because it teaches us about the relationship we should have with God. Judaism teaches that God has given us the world in order to develop it and improve upon it. The wheat is provided; it is up to us to turn it into bread. And yet we attribute the bread to its ultimate source: the One 'who brings *bread* from the earth.'"

My father would conclude, "Eating the Shabbat *challah* is a celebration of what human beings can do in this world. Bread reminds us of the simple yet deep path Judaism asks us to walk through life – the path of changing this world for the better."

This moment of celebration is tempered with salt as we pour a ritual amount on the bread. Haughtiness can creep into our hearts as our endeavors bear fruit. We change wheat into bread, cotton into cloth, atoms into nuclear reactors. The salt is symbolic of constriction. We need to constrict our ego and find a balance between our need to achieve and the imperative not to see ourselves as all-powerful.

Savoring Shabbat

*The higher you get spiritually, the closer you are to the earth
and every single human being on it*
(Rabbi Shlomo Carlebach)

O N SHABBAT we have long festive meals, and this is not only because
Jews love to eat. There actually is a point to all this food. Each Shabbat
meal is a mini-Passover *seder*. During the meal, thoughts concerning
the weekly Torah portion are shared and ancient poems are sung to
traditional tunes handed down over the generations.

Shabbat is the time to throw our diets out the window. According
to Jewish Law, one is supposed to have three meals on Shabbat. And
if you think we're talking about cucumbers and cottage cheese, you've
never been in a Jewish home!

We're talking about chicken soup with *matzah* balls, gefilte fish
with horseradish, noodle kugel with lots of raisins, roasted chicken, a
big green salad, plenty of *challah* and, of course, dessert. If you make
it through the first meal of the three, on Friday night, you get to enjoy
the second meal, Shabbat lunch – and that means *chulent. Chulent* is a
slow-cooking stew made of beans, barley, onions, meat and potatoes. It
has been simmering since Friday afternoon, and getting more delicious
with each passing hour.

Sweet noodle kugel. Sweet *challah* with poppy seeds and raisins.
Judaism is so sweet and so beautiful; it is meant to be served up and

shared. We need a Judaism with tastes and smells. A Judaism that conjures up memories of favorite times with *Bubby* and *Zeidy*. A Judaism that commands us to enjoy the sweet sleepiness that falls upon us after we finish a steaming bowl of *chulent*.

The food is an opportunity to gather with friends and family. It's not good to be alone on Shabbat. Families are expected to sit around a table and enjoy the togetherness. They are expected to bring in guests, even total strangers.

It is not always easy to be together, especially with family members, so we keep working on it week after week. Hopefully by next week, I'll learn not to insult my brother and I'll be more sensitive to my sister.

These long Shabbat meals are a good time for communication. A perfect time to say a *dvar Torah*, a word of Torah thought. Everyone shares his or her insights concerning the weekly Torah portion. Suddenly we have risen above our daily concerns and are grappling with issues like:

- Why did Cain kill Abel?
- Why did God use water, and not fire, to destroy the world during Noah's time?
- Why was it so important for the Jewish people to receive the Ten Commandments in a desert?
- What are the practical implications of, "Love your neighbor as you love yourself"?
  and…
- What are the universal messages of Judaism?

As the weekly Torah portion changes, so do the discussions. The intellectual richness is a source of pride in every home.

The Shabbat table becomes the Jewish melting pot. The hot chicken soup thaws us out towards each other. The words of Torah intrigue us and help us see new sides to the person sharing them. And don't forget the singing! Reb Nachman of Breslov teaches: "When we sing, it is not that we have broken through the walls that separate us.

When we sing, those walls do not even exist." For those few precious moments of song, we are one. We can touch each other, link arms and hold hands. We are living the Shabbat message of oneness.

Rabbi Shlomo Carlebach observed that the higher you go physically, the further you are from earth. Yet, he taught, the higher you get spiritually, the closer you are to the earth and every single human being on it.

The meal ends with a communal recital of *Birkat HaMazon*, the Grace After Meals. Each meal is a time of reconnecting to our heritage, our Jewish emotions and ideals. Come join us! Savor the sweetness of Judaism yourself!

Havdalah: Smelling the Sweetness

I will have trust and I will not be afraid

(from the *Havdalah* service)

𝑇T's SATURDAY NIGHT, the end of Shabbat, and my family is giving its weekly farewell to the Shabbat Queen and welcome to the new week. With the lights switched off, the flicker of the *Havdalah* candle is reflected in my children's eyes. The wine cup is full, the spice box is fragrant, and I begin to strum my guitar. It's *Havdalah*, time for the Shabbat to end.

A blessing is said, thanking God for creating spices, and the spice box is passed around. The smell is supposed to take us back to the first time the sense of smell was used: "And God formed man from the dust of the ground and breathed into his nostrils a soul of life" (Genesis 2:7). The first smell was the spiritual fragrance of the soul as God breathed it into the body.

The spices are like smelling salts as we begin to feel faint from the departure of our extra Shabbat soul. The spices awaken us spiritually, and suddenly we feel God breathing into us a new spirit. Every moment can be filled with spirituality. Every moment can smell so sweet.

We are transfixed by the multi-wick *Havdalah* candle flaming in the darkness. After the blessing is said, we hold up our fingers so that the fire's glow reflects off our nails. This is an act of hope, blessing ourselves and our children that we should utilize the fire of creativity to make the world a better place – a place where fire is used not to destroy, but to give warmth.

I look at my children as we sing the *Havdalah* service written so long ago: "Behold, God is powerful, savior; I will have trust and I will not be afraid...." Yet I do have fears; I am afraid for my children. I am afraid because the world is not always a spiritual place. And people do use fire to destroy, and people do forget that life is supposed to be sweet. My anxiety leads me to try to do the best parenting job I can, and the rest I turn over to God, my savior, who is powerful and will bring healing to this world.

Every Saturday night we sing the words of the *Havdalah* service and perform its rituals, in the hope that we can bring the spiritual awakening of the holy Shabbat into the coming week.

The Jewish Year

Elul

A Time for Closeness

*Elul is the time to come closer to those
with whom we are already close*
(Rabbi Shlomo Carlebach)

$\mathcal{E}$ LUL is the last month of the Jewish year. However, we experience it as a beginning. This is because it comes after the summer vacation and also because we spend this month doing intensive spiritual housecleaning to get ready for Rosh Hashanah. What spiritual awakening should we look for during the Jewish month of Elul? Elul is a month of forgiveness and renewed intimacy. During Elul, God forgave the Jewish people for worshiping the Golden Calf. But there was much more going on than Divine kindness. What did it mean when the people bowed down to that molten figure? In God's eyes it was nothing less than an act of adultery. God was a lover betrayed by a beloved. By forgiving them, God once again sought out the Jewish people for a close and intimate relationship.

Just as God sought to bring the Jewish people closer, so, too, are we expected to come closer to others. All those people I see on my way to work, on the bus, on the street; all my friends and family members – let's get close. If you're standing near someone as you commute to work, you can try to strike up a conversation. A minute ago you were light years apart; and now, now you are so much closer. Tomorrow when you see this person again, he won't be a stranger. A month from now you may even be friends.

That guy you're sitting next to on the plane – you know, the one who looks like he wants to talk. Why don't you ask him where he's from and where he's heading? He might help you figure out where you're heading, too. This is one of the reasons the Talmud teaches: "As you walk throughout this world, you should always be the first to say hello" (Ethics of the Fathers 4:15).

Just one hello and we are all so close; Elul is the month to do it.

On a deeper level, Rabbi Shlomo Carlebach taught that the internal work of Elul is to come closer to those with whom we are *already* close. It can be much easier to open up our hearts to people we barely know. But what about those who mean so much to us? Why is it easier to feel the pain of the poor people in Malaysia than it is the pain of my own sister?

You live with your children. You dedicate your time to them; you give them your money and your kisses. But how close are you really? You've lived with your partner for how many years? Then how come you feel so far apart? There is no one closer to us than our own parents. But we may not have spoken to them for months. I hurt them, and they hurt me. It's just too much to deal with.

This is the power of Elul – the power to bridge the gap with those closest to us. Elul gives us the strength to say: Let's try again. I know there's a history. I know it hurts. But God forgave the Jewish people and entered into an intimate relationship with them again, despite their betrayal. We can do the same.

On the deepest level, there is no other way. The destiny of the Jewish people is to be tied to God; that is the Divine plan. And so God took them back. We, too, have our own individual destinies. We, too, are tied: to our parents, our spouses and our children. We have no choice. We have to take them back.

Being so close, in one sense, and yet so far in another, is a common phenomenon in so many aspects of Judaism. We keep Shabbat, but does its holiness truly penetrate our souls? Do we come to realize that there is a whole other plane of existence beyond our mundane weekly one? Why is Shabbat still so far from us? We give charity, but does it alter our view of the material side of life? Does it imbue us with the knowledge that all wealth comes from above and is only a gift for us to share with others? Why are we so far removed from the act of *tzedakah* that we just performed?

We need to come closer, so much closer.

Therefore, the spiritual awakening of Elul begins with questions like these:

Whom am I far from?
What am I gaining by distancing myself from this person?
How do I need to change in order to come closer to this person?

There is another type of closeness that I call: Similarity is Proximity. You may be far away from another person, but you are close to each other because you are so much alike. Let's say my best friend is in Montana and I am in Pennsylvania. Although the distance is great, we feel close because we are so similar.

In the physical world, proximity is measured by physical distance. In the spiritual world, proximity is measured by similarity. How close am I to God? It all depends on how similar I am to God, how much I strive to act in God's ways and make myself over in God's image.

In relationships, we make a fundamental error. We think that if only the *other* person did this, that or the other, then we could be so much closer. Most of us carry around a mental shopping list of how we would like our friend, spouse or child to change.

I finally understood this when a colleague of mine, Tzvi Michael, explained to a group of college students how he met his wife. For a long time he'd been carrying around a list, in his firm resolution that he would only marry a woman who fulfilled all his requirements. Then he realized that any woman who *did* fulfill all his requirements would be so far developed that she would never want to marry *him*. It was then that he understood: In order to find a wife he had to first *become* his own list.

This is one of the deepest secrets of life. We become closer to people, not when *they* change the way we want them to – but when *we* make the change. Because similarity is proximity. As *we* become closer to who *we* want to be, we will inevitably become closer to all those around us.

An Untapped Source

Our deepest fear is not that we are inadequate.
Our deepest fear is that we are powerful beyond measure
(Nelson Mandela)

I LIKE READING horoscopes in the newspaper. Not that I actually believe in that stuff, but I'm enticed by the aura of knowing what will happen during the coming week. Even the Talmud speaks about the spiritual influence the stars have on our lives (Jerusalem Talmud *Shabbat* 156a).

Seeing that the Talmud establishes that the stars *do* influence our lives, the *Sfat Emet* – the chassidic master of Ger, (vol. 5, p. 136) – asks why Virgo is the astrological sign of Elul, the month preceding Rosh Hashanah.

His answer provides us with a deep spiritual awakening as to how we should perceive other people and ourselves. Approaching the Jewish New Year, we need the sign of Virgo because inside each of us there is an untouched, virgin place. No matter how old we are, there will always be an untapped source of youthfulness waiting to be found.

The Rebbe of Ger calls this place a *gan na'ul* and a *ma'ayan chatum* – a "locked garden" and a "sealed spring." During the month preceding Rosh Hashanah, we are trying to discover our locked garden and our sealed spring. As we reconnect to the inside of who we are, we find within ourselves a multi-hued garden fed by a surging spring.

Trying to tap into this pristine place is not a meditative act reserved for special individuals. The Rebbe of Ger was speaking to people like you and me.

A similar idea is found in another section of the Talmud (*Bava Kama* 97b). Here we find that Abraham and Sarah minted their own coins. One side of the coin read: "The Old Ones," and the other side read: "The Virgin and the Boy." Through their selfless acts for others, on both the physical and spiritual planes, Abraham and Sarah became known as "The Old Ones." This was an ancient expression denoting wisdom and respect. However, no matter how old they grew, they never left that first place of being virgins. They grew older in years, but never became emotionally or spiritually worn out.

Most people, as they go through life, become old and dried up on the inside. Yet, there are those spiritually-awakened few who remain youthful, always connected to the infinity within us – the place that knows no boundaries of time or space, no physical constraints. It's a place that gives strength: the strength to go beyond who we are; the strength to forgive; the strength to make room for others; the strength to hug and kiss those we find so hard to embrace.

As spiritual newborns we can once again taste the freshness of life.

Remember how joyful you were when your first child was born? And now that he doesn't want to take out the garbage, you fight and aren't quite so joyful. Close your eyes and awaken, now, as a new parent. This is the first time you have ever seen your son. It is so deep.

Remember how you danced at your wedding? Remember how you spun around and jumped till you were dizzy with joy? Close your eyes and awaken, now, as a newlywed. Feel again how much your wife means to you, how much you love your husband. Take your spouse's hand and dance with him or her. Spin around until you grow breathless and dizzy.

"Thank you, God, because each word of your Torah transforms me. Please allow me to always be feeling and tasting things for the first time." This is the spiritual awakening that the *Sfat Emet*, the Rebbe of Ger, was referring to.

A hundred years after the *Sfat Emet*, Nelson Mandela, in his inaugural address as president of South Africa, talked movingly about finding our inner selves:

> Our deepest fear is not that we are inadequate. Our deepest fear is that we are powerful beyond measure. It is our light, not our darkness, that most frightens us. We ask ourselves, who am I to be brilliant, gorgeous, talented and fabulous? Actually, who are you not to be? You are a child of God. Your playing small doesn't serve the world. There is nothing enlightened about shrinking so that other people won't feel insecure around you. We were born to make manifest the glory of God that is within us. It's not just in some of us; it's in everyone. And as we let our own light shine, we unconsciously give other people permission to do the same. As we are liberated from our own fear, our presence automatically liberates others.

Rabbi Shlomo Carlebach would frequently say that we are afraid of our own holiness, frightened of being who we can be.

Rosh Hashanah is a time of judgment, but not for the things we did wrong. We are judged for our misdeeds on Yom Kippur. Rosh Hashanah is a time of judgment for not being who we could have been during the past year.

We are given the gift of Elul, a whole month before Rosh Hashanah, to think about our answers to these difficult questions: Who am I and who can I be? Who can I be as I learn to connect to my innermost, infinite, virgin being?

Rosh Hashanah

Rosh Hashanah and The Lion King

And God said, "Let us make man so that he will rule…"

(Genesis 1:26)

Six years ago we disconnected our TV antenna for good. Now we only watch videos. Having kids and disconnecting the TV means that I have seen *The Lion King* about 300 times. I like Simba. I could go for a little "Hakuna Matata" in my life; just kick back, shake my mane in the wind and practice my pouncing.

In trying to prepare for Rosh Hashanah, I remembered something and decided to watch *The Lion King* for the 301st time. And I found a number of messages in *The Lion King* which are closely related to Rosh Hashanah.

Embarrassed by his past, Simba has decided to forget his upbringing and live a life of "Hakuna Matata" – no worries. Yet when Simba discovers that his pride is in dire peril, he finds himself in a dilemma: Should he continue enjoying his present lifestyle or return to his pride, which would mean facing his past?

Deep in thought, he wanders the savannah. It is there that he meets Rafiki, the mystic guru baboon. Rafiki dances around Simba, until Simba angrily blurts out, "Who are you?"

Rafiki shoots back, "The question is not who am I, but WHO ARE YOU?"

Head bowed, Simba admits, "I used to know, but I am not so sure anymore."

Judaism claims that on Rosh Hashanah we are like Simba. Life's twists and turns can make us forget who we are. We look at our lives and say, "How did I get here?" At times like this we feel utterly lost, even though we have degrees, a job, money in the bank, a car and a wide-band Internet connection.

Trying to remember who we are is the purpose of sitting in the synagogue for hours on Rosh Hashanah. Rosh Hashanah, the Jewish New Year, is also Adam and Eve's birthday. So, on the birthday of humanity, we sit in the synagogue and ask ourselves these spiritually awakening questions:

- Why were we created?
- What is our purpose in life?
- Am I where I want to be?

Both Rafiki and Judaism supply the answer.

Rafiki says to Simba, "You don't know who you are, but I do. You are Mufasa's boy."

Simba exclaims: "You knew my father!"

"Correction," says Rafiki, "I KNOW your father."

Simba: "I hate to tell you this, but he died a long time ago."

Rafiki: "Wrong again. He's alive and I will show him to you. Follow old Rafiki and I will show him to you."

Simba follows Rafiki through prickly thorns and strangulating vines (probably representing the difficult psychological journey into our past). They come out to a pool of water in the clearing.

Rafiki says, "Shhh, look down there," pointing to the pool.

Simba slowly approaches the pool and peers apprehensively into it, but turns away in disappointment, saying, "That's not my father. That's just my reflection in the water."

"No!" says Rafiki (now using his Indian Buddhist accent), "look harder." As Simba stares at his own reflection, the water shimmers and changes until it reflects back the face of his father, Mufasa.

Rafiki (still using his Indian Buddhist accent) says, "You see, he lives in you."

Now for some more Disney magic....

The clouds above the pool begin to churn and twist until they form a silhouette of Mufasa. Simba is having a vision.

Mufasa roars from the heavens: "Simba!"

Simba cries out: "Father!"

Mufasa (with a deep God/lion voice): "Simba, you have forgotten me."

Simba: "No, how could I?"

Mufasa: "You have forgotten who you are and so you have forgotten me. Look inside yourself, Simba; you are more than what you have become. You must take your place in the circle of life."

Simba replies: "How can I go back? I am not who I used to be."

Mufasa, echoing as he begins to fade, "Remember who you are. You are my son and the one true king. Remember who you are. Remember!"

Simba must realize that inside of him, he has kingship and the potential for greatness.

Judaism's answer to Simba's confession – "I used to know who I was, but I'm not so sure anymore" – is almost the same.

The Bible clearly states that human beings were created to govern and take care of the world. "And God said, 'Let us make man so that he may rule the fish of the sea, the birds of the sky, the livestock animals, and all the earth'" (Genesis 1:26).

Rosh Hashanah and *The Lion King* share a common perception of who we are. Both God and Mufasa believe that we are sons and daughters of the one true king. With this in mind, Rosh Hashanah becomes a time for us to consider how we are going to take our place in the circle of life. A time to ask ourselves: Are we going to take on the mantle of leadership (in our case, the responsibility for what goes on in this world)?

Simba decides he cannot continue living his "Hakuna Matata" existence. He returns to his pride, faces the mistakes of his past, fights for victory and takes his place in the circle of life.

Will we do the same?

Putting the Pieces Back Together

As much as I want You to be responsive to my needs,
I need You, God, to listen to my pain

(Psalms 130:2, a free translation)

"*A*BBA, look at this!"

I look up and see Shayna, my eight-year-old daughter, standing in front of me with her arms outstretched. She displays her first work from the ceramic club, a clay *shofar* painted brown with three thin blue stripes. I carefully hold the *shofar* and marvel at her workmanship.

I am happy that Shayna is happy. She is so totally engrossed in her happiness that I feel her enthusiasm lighting up her face and mine, too. I gently hand back the *shofar*, and with a spring in her walk, Shayna places it on the table. But in her excitement, she miscalculates the distance. The *shofar* lands on the table, slides off and smashes on the floor. The clay *shofar* is now in a thousand pieces.

I think to myself, "Ooooh noooo!" I look at Shayna and she, too, is in a thousand pieces. She walks over to the corner of the living room, sits on the last seat of the sofa and begins to cry. My mind pulses with the recurring thought, "Oh no, oh no, oh no. My poor Shayna, her heart is a thousand times broken."

I go over, sit next to her, put my arms around her and hold her as she weeps.

In the past, I would have said "Shhh, shhh, Shayna. It'll be okay.

Don't worry, it'll be okay." Yet I feel that this is not the right response. I have found that parents have a wonderful, natural drive to protect their children, even if it means saying, "It'll be okay," when we have no idea at all if it really will be. Maybe saying, "It'll be okay," is actually belittling what happened.

Silently, I hold her and think about a teaching of King David. In Psalm 130:2, King David says: "As much as I want You to be responsive to my needs, I need You, God, to listen to my pain" (a free translation).

So I listen to Shayna cry and hope that by doing so I am giving her the comfort she needs. As I hold Shayna, my father-in-law – who is visiting for the High Holy Days – is busy picking up the larger clay pieces. He collects them, lays them all on the table and goes down to the basement. He returns with my tool chest, takes out the Superglue and begins the slow, laborious task of pasting the *shofar* back together. He spends many hours employing great skill, and he is successful.

As I prepare for Rosh Hashanah, I find myself thinking about Shayna's *shofar*. For as I approach the Days of Judgment, I enter into a process of self-evaluation. Recalling my mistakes makes me feel that my life, too, is in a thousand pieces. I feel tears welling up as I recall those parts of my life that could have become pieces of art, yet instead are shards of shattered clay. Those life energies that could have brought light to my life, but instead were wasted. I, too, turn to my heavenly parent, and ask God not to tell me that everything is going to be okay. Rather, I say: Could You please put Your arm around me and hold me tight, as I feel the anguish my mistakes are causing me?

And, if, God, by some miracle, You happen to have a spare angel around, could You send it down with some holy glue to piece my life back together again?

The Secret of the
Three Shofar Blasts

I am not crying because it hurts so much,
but because it means so much

(Rabbi Shlomo Carlebach)

ANNETTE STARED at me and said, "You're not going to give them a *shofar* as a wedding gift, are you?"

I looked at the *shofar* I was holding and said, "A *shofar* is exactly what a new couple needs. The blowing of the *shofar* on Rosh Hashanah is all about celebrating and mending relationships. What better wedding gift?"

Although Annette agreed with me, we ended up giving our friends both a *shofar and* a crock pot.

Why was I so insistent?

Because I know how much the sounds of the *shofar* have helped Annette and me to open our hearts to each other – how this biblical musical instrument, a simple ram's horn, has been mending relationships throughout history, piercing into the deepest recesses of the soul.

We need the *shofar*. We need to learn the art of how to blow it and how to hear it being blown. And we need to teach this art to our children and to their children, throughout the generations. There are three different blasts we blow on the *shofar*: *tekiah*, *shevarim*, *teruah*. What is the spiritual awakening that we gain from these *shofar* blowings?

The *tekiah* opens the gates of celebration. It is the loud, proud blast celebrating life and loving relationships: between couples, families and friends. The *tekiah* cries out, "I love you, I love you and I thank you for being with me." The *tekiah* awakens us to all the good that exists in our human and Divine relationships.

The three short, hesitating blows – known as *shevarim* – are the sighs of life, its hardships and tensions. Every relationship has its ups and downs, and therefore, at times, we feel a little broken. As we hear the *shevarim*, which actually means "brokenness," we need to learn how to be broken together with others and not close ourselves off from others when our life sours.

Rabbi Shlomo Carlebach taught, "The question is not how much you love someone when you love each other. The question is how much do you love that person when you hate each other. The question is not how much you love God when you're feeling close. The question is how fast do you run back to God after you've done something wrong."

These *shevarim* sighs come from our mistakes. The *shevarim* blasts want us to share each other's troubles so that we can carry the weight of life together.

The *shofar* blowing ends with nine weeping blasts, which shatter our heart. This is the sound of the *teruah*. My lack of consideration and selfishness have soiled my relationships. And I don't deserve a second chance. So I'm begging you: Please take me back, because I am beyond brokenness, I am just shattered pieces. And it hurts. It hurts so much.

The *teruah* wants us to open our hearts and realize how much we have damaged our connections with our partners, our children, our friends and our God. This is a weeping sound that opens the heart, and we cry with it. Yet the sounds of the *teruah* should pierce our heart, not out of sadness, but because we love the other person so much and we're so sorry we've caused him or her anguish during this past year. This is what I think Rabbi Shlomo Carlebach meant when he would say, "I am not crying because it hurts so much, but because it *means* so much."

This ritual of blowing the *shofar* becomes even more meaningful when we learn that the law calls for the *tekiah*, the blast of love, to be blown before and after every *shevarim* and every *teruah*. Because no matter what has happened in the relationship, we do love each other. And God loves us too. The *tekiah* – before and after the sigh and before and after the shatteredness – is our prayer, "Love me even though you know how my mistakes have blackened my soul." The *tekiah* is our cry: "Hold me. Hold me. Hold me in my utter shatteredness. Hold me as I try to put the pieces back together."

Annette and I, like many couples, have had times of *tekiah*, times of *shevarim* and times of *teruah*. We've been through love, brokenness and even shatteredness.

Let us all remember to blow a *tekiah*, a blast of celebration, before and after every *shevarim* and every *teruah*.

Rosh Hashanah:
The Birthday of the World

The spiritual birthday of every single human being

$\mathcal{D}$ID YOU ever hear of Farrell's?

Farrell's was a western-style ice cream parlor where my parents took us for birthdays. Birthdays at Farrell's were great. I remember sitting around a wooden table with a checked tablecloth, when out would come six waiters: one ringing an old fashion fireman's bell, one banging on a drum, and four carrying a wooden stretcher – two at the front and two at the back. In the middle of this stretcher rested a huge tub of Farrell's ice cream. As they placed the tub on the table the six waiters would sing in unison: "Happy birthday to you...."

What made Farrell's birthdays so great – beyond the ice cream and the hoopla – was that they made you feel special. As we grow older and no longer go to Farrell's, we still get a kick out of a card, an e-mail or phone message singing: "Happy birthday to you. Happy birthday to you [add the music]. Happy birthday dear [add the name]. Happy birthday to you!"

We think to ourselves: "Yeah! I'm still special."

So why is it that as we get older, we begin to dread birthdays? Why do we feel such a heavy weight with each passing year? Rabbi Aryeh Ben David says: "Birthdays are only significant when your life isn't."

Birthdays remind us that another year has passed. If, during that year, we have grown emotionally, if we have lived meaningful lives, if we have a clear picture of where we are going, and are continuing on our journey of spiritual awakening, then our birthdays are not going to shake us up. They will either pass uneventfully, or be felt as a happy day to reflect upon how good the year has been.

However, if we really don't feel our lives are on track and our job is basically going nowhere, then our birthday reminds us that during the past year, nothing has changed and maybe nothing ever will. Then we surely don't want to be reminded that it's our birthday.

When we were children, birthdays made us feel special because of external stimuli – because of ice cream on stretchers and singing waiters. As we grow older, birthdays only make us feel special if our lives truly are.

What's Rosh Hashanah? Rosh Hashanah is the birthday of the world, the spiritual birthday of every single human being.

The depth and spirituality of life presents us with profound challenges and expectations. If we've lived up to our expectations during the past year, then Rosh Hashanah is a happy day. However, if we haven't met the challenges presented to us, Rosh Hashanah can be a terrifying experience.

That's why Rosh Hashanah can be perceived as a day of judgment, although in truth, it's a day of spiritual awakening. If I've worked on awakening spiritually, if I've done my spiritual homework, then Rosh Hashanah will be easy. It's my birthday and I want to make an accounting of where I've gotten. This is the judgment of Rosh Hashanah.

But most of us don't want to be judged. We also don't want to judge ourselves. Yet we need to know that the judgment is being done with love. God is saying, "I love you so much. I have such high expectations of you. And I know you can grow more; expand your heart more."

Rabbi Shlomo Carlebach taught that on Rosh Hashanah two movies are played in the heavenly theater. One movie shows what we have done in the past year. The second movie shows what we could have done. The closer the two movies are to each other, the better. When they match, you're in heaven. So I bless us all that our movies match – and that we give each other the strength to live up to the grand hopes life holds out for us.

Oh, and by the way, happy birthday!

God-Given Beginnings

All beginnings are difficult

THERE ARE TWO WAYS for us to reach our potential. One is to stop repeating the acts which take us further away from who we want to be. But there is another way: Instead of focusing on our mistakes, we can focus on our beginnings. As soon as we fix our beginnings, everything else falls into place.

Rabbi Shlomo Carlebach taught that Rosh Hashanah is not a time for cleaning. Only on Yom Kippur is God's Laundromat open. Rosh Hashanah is a time for beginnings. Rosh Hashanah is an opportunity to spiritually awaken and give ourselves a new beginning.

The saddest thing is when we say: I'll be the same tomorrow as I am now, because that's the way I was yesterday. We begin to believe we can't change. We should say to ourselves: No! It's Rosh Hashanah, the beginning of a new year! I have the right to a new beginning!

As children, we started out happy, energetic, creative, helpful, curious, spiritual and pure. In Judaism, we believe that these are our God-given beginnings. Rosh Hashanah is a time to go back and think: Where and when did I stray from the path? Who am I, really?

This process is called *teshuvah*, which means return. Return to where? Return to our beginnings. To the time before all the mistakes were made. In Judaism, there is only one place to return to, and that place is our holy essence. When we recognize that our essence is holy, we are able to listen to the holy messages we have inside. Messages like: Do good; be helpful; love; forgive; create; help others shine; and, don't be afraid to shine yourself.

Fixing our beginnings is difficult work. Either we're still focused on our past mistakes or we're trying to start afresh but not looking in the right place. This is why Rosh Hashanah is two days long. We need to spend two days in a spiritual house, a synagogue, in order to begin again.

What is my essence? How do I want to express my essence in my daily life? How do I want to express my essence in my relationships, at home and at work? These are a few of the questions presented to us on this holiday. These questions may be hard to ask and even harder to answer, but I think they are the questions that can take us one step closer to opening up the door to a fresh start.

As we learn to give ourselves new beginnings, we will also be able to do the same for others. Rosh Hashanah then becomes a time to grant others a clean slate. It is true that such-and-such happened between us, but garbage is not something we should hold in our heart. It's something we should get rid of before it starts to rot and spoil everything around it. If you want to have a spiritual awakening on Rosh Hashanah, turn to the people closest to you and say: Let's start all over again! Let's give each other a new beginning!

Yom Kippur

Surely You Need Something Fixed!

If I am tomorrow as I am today,
for what do I have a tomorrow?

(The Rebbe of Kotsk)

DURING THE DAYS between Rosh Hashanah and Yom Kippur, we engage rigorously in the spiritual awakening called *teshuvah*. *Teshuvah* is the process of evaluating who we are and taking stock of how we have acted during the past year.

Soon we will spend all of Yom Kippur day reciting prayers which direct us towards rejuvenation through discarding our mistakes and imperfections.

By the end of Yom Kippur we will feel much lighter, because we will not have to carry our mistakes with us into the New Year. If we are truly sincere and make good on our promises to do better, God will forgive us for what we have done in the past. Our sincere regret, combined with God's forgiveness, will truly enable us to "throw out the garbage."

Teshuvah means *return*. What are we returning to? To our most essential self. To the self which existed before I made all the mistakes. To the college-age self who still believed in changing the system. To the teenage self who still believed with fiery intensity in truth, love and honesty. And to the childhood self who only wanted to be good and please others.

Our mistakes coat us with so many lies and so much deception that we begin to forget what we really believe in. So now we are trying to peel off those layers and return to the essence. As the chassidic master, the Rebbe of Kotsk, would often say, "If I am tomorrow as I am today, for what do I have a tomorrow?"

The nineteenth-century chassidic master, Reb Levi Yitzhak of Berditchev, saw the best in everyone around him. Yet he always felt that he himself had much to improve.

In his town there lived a shoemaker with a large family. They never had enough money, so the shoemaker was always looking for more work to do. Sometimes he would walk through the streets, seeking people who needed their shoes fixed.

It happened one day that the Rebbe was standing at the doorway of his home when the shoemaker passed by. "Rebbe!" cried the shoemaker. "Surely you have something that needs fixing?"

When he heard these words, Reb Levi Yitzchak turned white. He raised his hands to his face and began to weep. Turning to his wife, he sighed: "You see, even a simple shoemaker can tell that I need to fix myself!" For Reb Levi Yitzchak, even the words of a cobbler were a spiritual awakening.

The Road Home

Return one day before you die
(Ethics of the Fathers 12:2)

BEFORE HIS DEATH, Moses stood up in front of the Jewish people and said, "You know, it was only an eleven-day walk from Mount Sinai to where we are standing today, at the border of the Land of Israel. But it took us forty years to get here!" (Deuteronomy 1:3)

Moses was trying to teach the Jewish people that had they stayed focused on their goal of coming home, it would have taken just eleven days. Then, as now, coming home was not an easy thing to do.

How long does it take for me to get home?

Today, at the age of thirty-seven, it takes me around thirty to forty minutes. Had you asked me when I was in my teens, the answer would have been quite different.

Coming home is not so simple. We don't always feel comfortable at home. We can be hauling heavy baggage along with our suitcases. I may not get along with my mother or father, brother or sister. There may be issues that need to be dealt with, and, until they are, the road home may be unbearably winding and long.

But let's say you find out your sister is seriously ill. Then you'd be home in an hour. You haven't spoken to your father in five years, but you hear he has cancer and you're on the next plane.

Suddenly, it's easy to come home.

The distance disappears and you find yourself close by. You say to yourself: I have to get home.

That's all. It's not complicated any more. It's simple.

Now imagine you come home, not because anyone's sick, but because you have cut through all the nonsense that is separating you from the people you love the most.

How do you cut through?

Sometimes you need to travel all the way around the world to find out there's no place like home.

Sometimes you have to try out every hair-do and fashion item to find out you just want to look like yourself.

Sometimes you have to imitate TV sitcoms and famous comedians to find out you just need to be you.

How do you achieve spiritual awakening? How do you cut through?

You need to focus.

The Sages teach: "Return one day before you die" (Ethics of the Fathers 12:2).

The Sages are saying: Imagine you have six months to live. How would you spend that time, and with whom would you spend it? Now imagine you have only eleven days. Now imagine you have only one day.

Six months.

Eleven days.

One day to return.

Return to that which is really essential in your life.

Return to your family.

Return to your friends.

Return to your dreams.

Return to your life.

And most of all – return home. It can take forty years...or eleven days.

The Yom Kippur Bike

Yom Kippur is when I emulate God
by learning to give a second chance

I RECENTLY SPENT a summer at Northeastern University in downtown Boston, finishing a degree in counseling. I had never been to Boston before and I really wanted to see this beautiful city. Good friends of mine lent me their bike and off I went.

Northeastern is centrally located, so I could ride almost anywhere within thirty minutes – north to Brookline or south to Chinatown and Harvard Square. Unfortunately, I didn't get too far. Within the first half-hour, the bike was stolen. Not only were my sightseeing days now over, but I had to face my friends and tell them about the bike. They took it pretty well, assuring me that their insurance would probably cover the loss.

About a week after the bike was stolen, my friend came over to visit. I met him outside my dorm house, Kerr Hall, and there he was with a brand new set of wheels.

"Here," he said, "I got you another bike."

I thanked him over and over, and, as he hurried off to work, I took my new bike for a ride. I rode down Huntington to Mass Avenue, over the Charles River towards Harvard Square. As I rode, I kept thinking how nice it was of him to give me another chance. I veered past the Prudential building and the Christian Science center and suddenly it became clear to me: I was riding on a Yom Kippur bike!

Do you know when it was that God gave the Jewish people the Second Tablets? It was on Yom Kippur. Imagine: God was going to share with the Jewish people the ten most important truths of life, known as the Ten Commandments. Moses had been on Mount Sinai for forty days, learning about these truths so that he could teach them to his people. But the Jewish people weren't home. They were out partying with the Golden Calf. They weren't ready to receive them, so the tablets were broken.

The next morning the people saw the pieces of what could have been, the two tablets broken into a thousand fragments. They realized what an opportunity they had lost and they, too, were broken. They begged for forgiveness, but they were not forgiven so easily.

However, the Jewish people didn't give up. For forty days they searched their hearts and cried over their loss. And, after forty days, God forgave them and let Moses come back up to Mount Sinai. But God waited yet another forty days, culminating in Yom Kippur, until it was time to give the Jewish people the Second Tablets. If God had already forgiven them, why was there a need to wait another forty days?

The answer is that as hard as forgiving is, there is something which is even harder, and that is giving someone a second chance.

If you hurt me, I may be able to forgive you, but I'm not going to trust you with my feelings and secrets.

God forgave the Jewish people, then waited another forty days to give them a second chance – to once again put trust in them, to be open again to the possibility of being hurt by them. That is what happened on Yom Kippur, and that is the essence of the day. Not the forgiveness that already took place forty days before, but the reestablishment of the relationship.

Yom Kippur is when I emulate God by learning to trust once again, by learning to give a second chance.

I will always be grateful to my dear, dear friend, for giving me a taste of Yom Kippur as I rode over the Charles River on my Yom Kippur bike.

Sukkot

Material Possessions: Do I Own Them or Do They Own Me?

By always viewing life in the small screen of the computer
I lose sight of the awesomeness of the heavens

THE STORY goes that in the early 1900s, a Jewish immigrant in Manhattan took some boards and put up a *sukkah* in front of his apartment building. His neighbors were very upset with him, but although they tried, they could not convince him to take down his rickety little booth. Finally, the day before the holiday, they decided to take him to court. The judge listened to both sides and decided that clearly, the man must dismantle his booth, no two ways about it.

However, Judge Goldberg gave him eight days to do so!

For literally thousands of years Jews have been erecting *sukkahs* outside their homes, in memory of the huts our ancestors erected as they traveled through the desert. This is based on Leviticus 23:42: "During these seven days you must live in *sukkahs*.... This is so that future generations will know that I had the Israelites live in huts when I brought them out of Egypt."

When I decide to live in a *sukkah* for seven days, I come to a profound spiritual awakening. I begin to rethink my attitude toward my possessions. As I live in this hut I ask myself: Do my possessions enslave me and tie me down, or do they allow me to be free and do what I need to do?

Leaving my home and living in the same simple structure in which all my fellow Jews are living, I can sample a taste of the World to Come in which there will be equality among all people: no more mansions for some and hovels for others.

As I sit under my *sukkah*'s covering of branches, I ask myself: What truly gives me shelter in this world? Is it only my physical roof, or is there a Heavenly component in the fact that I have made it safely to this day? Gazing at the heavens through the branches helps me gain a clearer picture of what truly gives me protection. Or as contemporary people would say: By always viewing life in the small screen of the computer, I lose sight of the awesomeness of the heavens.

Journeying along a desert road, you come to understand what material possessions you really need in life. If I could sleep under the stars for forty years, would I need any other adornments in my home? If I knew I'd have to pick up and continue traveling at any moment, would I hold on to any but the barest essentials?

As you prepare to move out to your *sukkah* for the week, look around your home and ask yourself: All these clothes that stuff my closets, all these furnishings that fill my rooms, all these appliances that crowd my counters – do I own them or do they own me?

Spiritual Cities

May peace exist at your outer border
for only then will tranquility permeate your inner palace
(Psalms 122:7, a free translation)

*H*ow do you measure the spirituality of a city?

Do you count the special people who live there? The ones who help the sick and poor, open their homes to the hungry and lonely, and spend time in prayer for the welfare of the city's inhabitants?

Do you count the synagogues, churches and mosques? Do you stand outside the windows of these edifices and measure the depth of feeling in the words cried out there?

Do you make a list of the charitable groups and volunteer organizations?

I have a different way to gauge a city's spirituality, and it consists of asking one simple question:

Can a fourteen-year-old girl walk home safely in the middle of the night?

How safe are the streets of your city?

How safe are the parks during the day, and at night? How safe are the corridors of the local high school? The decisive question becomes not, "What do we do in our homes?" but rather, "Do our values and ethics flow out of our homes and become part of the neighborhood within which we live?"

On Sukkot, we are commanded to live in a spiritual building, a *sukkah*, for seven days. Sitting in our makeshift *sukkahs*, eating, singing, learning and sleeping, with the wind blowing through the branches and the sounds of the neighborhood filtering in, we must ask ourselves: How safe is it for me to sleep outside?

As we build our *sukkahs* outside our homes, we take a physical step outside, into our community. We take for granted that our communities will be safe enough for us and our children to sleep outside. We expect that its members will not harm us in the darkness of the night.

For this we strive: to build and live in such communities.

May we be successful that next year there will be more safe places on this earth, and that one day it will be safe enough all around the globe so that everyone in the world will be able to sleep outside.

As King David taught: "May peace exist at your outer border, for only then will tranquility permeate your inner palaces" (Psalms 122:7, a free translation).

Dancing As If No One Can See You

When I pray, I would love to spin like a top and fly like a bird

SIMCHAT TORAH is approaching and my thoughts turn to dancing. I like to dance at home with my kids. Dancing with my kids is special because there's no show, no embarrassment – just moving to the music. It's what I call: Dancing-As-If-No-One-Can-See-You. This kind of dancing is the most authentic expression of how the music touches you deep inside.

How do you teach your kids to dance as if no one can see them? It's simple. First, you, yourself, have to be able to dance as if no one can see you. Just allow the rhythm to lift your limbs and swing them this way and that.

I have the great fortune of belonging to a synagogue that has lots of dancing during prayers. Yet, when I dance there, I don't feel as free. Why? Because people are watching. Or because I think people are watching. And I'm scared they'll think I'm weird. And if they think I'm weird, they won't respect me anymore. So I hold back.

Really, when I pray, I would love to spin like a top and fly like a bird. And I know that as long as I hold back, I am not learning the lesson King David learned 3,000 years ago. In the tenth century B.C.E.,

King David made two attempts to bring the Ark of the Covenant from Samaria to Jerusalem. Both times there was dancing, but the first attempt failed while the second succeeded. Why was the second attempt to bring the ark successful?

It all had to do with the dance.

While the Ark of the Covenant was being paraded up to Jerusalem, King David led all the people in a dance. During his first attempt, King David wore his royal robes; the second time, he put on an *ephod* – the plain robe worn by the priests when they did their work in the Temple. In the second attempt, he changed his dance as well. Instead of the sedate two-step he did the first time, King David began spinning around with all his might, leaping up into the air.

Imagine!

King David was leading the multitudes of his nation to the holy city, and he was basically break-dancing! Why were these changes critical in gaining God's favor, enabling the ark to be brought to its rightful resting place?

The answer is that when King David took off his royal robes and changed into the simple dress of a Temple priest – when he break-danced instead of dancing in a slow shuffle – he was stripping away the dignity of his office and breaking through to his spiritual core. It is that sort of dance that God loves. It is then that God says, "You are now ready to hold the ark and ascend the holy mountain. You're the one I want in My parade."

King David had connected to his inner core. He was dancing as if no one was watching. I believe that many people are waiting to dance as if no one is watching.

We get so stiff as we grow up. But then a miracle happens when the music plays and we hold a child's hand. We begin to copy the child's dance movements. We allow ourselves to loosen up for the child's sake, but really, we enjoy it too. At last, we are reconnecting to our own inner child – the child that wants to jump, leap, spin, skip, hop and sing praises for the happiness welling up inside.

King David broke through. We can break through, too. This

Simchat Torah, it's just us and the Torah; just us expressing our love for the precious gift God has given us. We can take the Torah scroll in our arms and dance like a child. We can jump and leap and spin and skip and hop and sing praises as we cause our own Ark of the Covenant to ascend the holy mountain. We can close our eyes and let ourselves free. Indeed, if we wish, we can dance as if no one can see us.

Chanukah

The Day Michael Jackson Came to Synagogue

For me a life of only physical pursuits is like a death sentence
(Psalms 104:29, a free translation)

$\mathcal{B}$ELIEVE IT or not, Michael Jackson went to a Friday night service at the Carlebach synagogue in Manhattan. It was startling to see him spinning to the *niggunim,* and he even wore a black hat and black pants in order to fit in better. Do you want to know why he's so interested in Judaism? The answer is: Spiritual Awakening.

Michael is asking some serious questions: Who am I? Why am I alive? Why was I created? What is my purpose? And he, along with Madonna, Roseanne Barr, Goldie Hawn and many other people are turning to spirituality for answers. What all these people have figured out is what King David discovered in the tenth century B.C.E.: "For me a life of only physical pursuits is like a death sentence" (free translation of Psalms 104:29).

Now that there are Kabbalah centers and spirituality weekend retreats all over America and Europe, does this mean that Jewish educators can go on vacation? The answer is intrinsically connected to the holiday of Chanukah.

Chanukah means dedication. Chanukah is the holiday when we celebrate dedication to our spiritual values. It was during Chanukah that a group of Jews called the Maccabees said, "Our spiritual life is so important to us that we value it over our physical existence!"

When the Greek Empire came to Judea and said, "You can continue to live as long as you give up your Judaism and adopt a Hellenistic lifestyle," the answer was, "No!"

The Greeks said, "Then we will come and kill you." And the Maccabees answered, "Then we will fight back."

Why were the Jews willing to fight? Why were they willing to give up their lives?

The words of Dr. Martin Luther King, Jr. explain their heroic effort. In one of his public rallies, he said:

> They may hit you and they may kill you, but there are some things worth dying for. And I submit to you today that if a man has not found something worth dying for, he isn't fit to live.

The Hebrew word *Chanukah* means dedication: dedication to my spiritual path, even if it means testing my resolve. The heroes of Chanukah are saying that Jewish educators can go on vacation when only Jews around the world have internalized their Jewishness to such a degree that life without Judaism is no life at all.

This is the question that Chanukah lays before us: Is there anything you value so much that without it your life would not be worth living?

What is dedication?

During the wedding ceremony, the groom declares to his bride, "*Harei at mekudeshet li betaba'at zo* – "Behold you are dedicated and sanctified to me with this ring."

The married couple are forbidden to have relations with others, for they have dedicated themselves to each other. This is an emotional dedication: I have feelings for you which I have for no one else in the world. It is also a physical dedication: From now on, I dedicate my physical passion to you and you alone. This life of physical dedication is more than just not acting on a sexual attraction toward another person;

it is a channeling of one's sexual desires to a higher place. This is the place where my sexual passion becomes an expression of commitment, of intimate feelings and of a deep trust between the married couple.

The importance of dedicating and channeling one's physical passion was one of the fundamental arguments the Maccabees had with Greek culture. Hellenism was a culture of passion, expressed through art, music, drama, philosophy, sports, food orgies and battle. However, the Hellenists were not willing to dedicate their passion to God. That was the fundamental difference between them and the Jews. Judaism is a religion of passion, yet we are constantly trying to bring Godliness into our lives and seek those actions which will raise our passions to a spiritual level.

To a great extent, the Greek ethos was synonymous with hedonism. The Id was allowed to reign freely through sexual infidelity, gorging oneself with food and revelling in the bloody death of gladiators in the arena. In contrast, Judaism teaches us to channel our desires to conform to a Divine code of ethics.

Food? Yes, but only when it meets the deeply spiritual and ethical standards of *Kashrut*; and only after the proper blessing has been said; and only in amounts that promote health; and only in order to be strong to serve our Creator.

Sex? Yes, but only after you have dedicated your sexual relationship to one special person; and only according to the dictates of family purity; and only with modesty and dignity.

Beautiful clothing? Yes, but letting it all hang out is not a Jewish ideal. Be *attractive*, not *attracting*!

Money? Yes, but be sure to tithe for the poor.

Use your time as you see fit? Yes, but dedicate one day a week – Shabbat – to God.

Chanukah means dedication.

It is by the light of the *menorah* that the Maccabees transmitted the message of this holiday. For this candelabrum was never meant merely to emit a physical light, but rather to shine a spiritual light on our deepest (and at times darkest) passions.

If you are a passionate person, and at times your passions lead you to act in ways that you deem unworthy, then this is the holiday for you. On Chanukah, you need not keep your passions in check. You can allow them to fly to their highest source by channeling them to a loftier purpose.

This is a holiday of light, spiritual light, and there is nothing that gives a person more light than to say: I have only beauty inside myself. I just need to learn how to express my inner beauty in a beautiful way.

I bless you that you should stand by your candles and have the deepest spiritual awakening. I bless you that you should allow the Chanukah lights to enter and illuminate the deepest recesses of your soul.

Is It Christmas in There or Chanukah?

I would shine a great light into his heart
(Reb Zusha)

WE LIVE IN A SOCIETY where the Christmas season overpowers Chanukah. But there is still something we can do. Our family lights two Chanukah *menorahs* – one inside the house and another outside the front door. The one inside the house is for us to enjoy, but the one outside the door is even more important.

You see, there was a time when many Jews found more meaning in the Greek culture around them than they found in their own. They dressed like the Greeks, joined in their sporting events and social gatherings, and even had their circumcisions surgically altered so as not to look different in the gymnasium locker room.

However, the Maccabees found beauty and light and the deepest secrets of life in their Judaism. And they wanted everyone to know it. They therefore instituted the ancient tradition of lighting our *menorahs* outside the house in order to share this message with others.

Sadly, history repeats itself, and once again there are Jews who find more light in foreign cultures than they do in their own.

Part of the blame goes to teachers who spend their time saying,

"Do this," and "Don't do that." Rabbi Shlomo Carlebach helped me formulate a different path in Jewish education.

He used to tell the story of Reb Zusha, who asked the Seer of Lublin, "How would you help a person change his ways?" The Seer answered, "I'd take out the *Shulchan Aruch*, the Code of Jewish Law, and show him that what he was doing was wrong."

"Do you think that would bring the person close?" Reb Zusha replied. "On the contrary! It would only make him feel bad. And if he felt bad, he would run away from you."

The Seer nodded. "Rebbe," he asked, "how would you do it?"

To which Reb Zusha replied, "I would shine a great light into his heart, and show him the love that God has for every human being."

When you light the *menorah* in your home, you become one of those Jews who let the light of Judaism into their lives. When you light your *menorah* in a window or outside your door, you strive to share that light with others, reaching out to every Jew walking down the street. For there are many Jews looking into windows and into doorways to see if it's Christmas in there, or Chanukah.

Continuing the Miracle

The light that the Maccabees lit has lasted 2,200 years

OUR STAFF at Camp Moshava was so intent on creating an Israeli ambience that no one remembered to bring along a flag in order to celebrate the American bicentennial. Luckily, early in the morning of July 4, 1976, someone went out and came back with an American flag. We raised it with pride, but within the hour, the U.S. flag was gone and replaced with an Israeli one.

Now, this was not a case of a youthful overdose of Zionist enthusiasm. That day, when all of America was celebrating two hundred years of freedom, we at Camp Moshava were celebrating the release of seventy Jewish hostages from terrorist hands. That very day, Israeli commandos had flown from Israel over hostile African states to Entebbe, Uganda. Out of a Hercules plane rolled a replica of Idi Amin Dada's presidential limousine, loaded with Israeli soldiers. They drove up to the terminal where Arab and German terrorists were holding a group of Jews, killed the terrorists, loaded the hostages onto the plane and flew back to Israel.

It was a modern-day miracle. We danced and sang and were so proud to be a part of the Jewish people.

But what was the real miracle? Ingenious military strategy? Success against great odds? Yes, all true.

However, there was much more to this miracle. And that was that the Israeli soldiers cared enough about the Jewish people that they were willing to risk their lives for them. The miracle was that the Jewish state proved itself to be the protector of Jews everywhere.

Jewish history is overflowing with miracles, but they are of a very special kind. Few and far between are the miracles where God's hand is openly revealed. But many are the miracles that come through human conduits.

For God to perform a miracle is not so very hard. But for a human being to become a vessel of the miraculous – well, that is very difficult, indeed.

In Jewish history there are two miracle mountains: Mount Sinai, where the Ten Commandments were given, and Mount Moriah, where Abraham prepared to sacrifice his beloved son, Isaac.

Rabbi Joseph Soloveitchik asked: Which mountain in Jewish tradition has more significance? Clearly, we would think, Mount Sinai. Has there ever been a greater event in human history than the revelation of the ten basic principles of morality – principles which have shaped the development of all Western cultures?

Yet Mount Sinai has no religious significance in Judaism. And in fact, nobody really knows where it is. According to a midrash, all the mountains in the world vied for the honor, and God chose the lowliest, most humble mountain. Mount Sinai was certainly *not* the towering peak that carries its name today.

Rabbi Soloveitchik continued: God chose Mount Moriah as the place of the holy Temple, not Mount Sinai. Why? Because on Mount Sinai, God came down to the Jewish people. But on Mount Moriah, Abraham and Isaac raised themselves up to a Godly level. They took on the miraculous when they sacrificed their hearts and souls to the spiritual path that God set before them.

On Chanukah God performed a miracle: The *menorah* gave light for eight days using an amount of oil that wasn't sufficient even for one day.

But there is an even greater miracle: the small but determined light that the Maccabees lit has lasted 2,200 years. Each generation has passed down the Maccabean torch, and with it we light the *menorah*.

What was it about the Maccabean effort that has kept their torch burning for so long?

One can look to the actions of the Entebbe commandos for an answer. The Maccabees dedicated their very lives to the physical, spiritual and cultural continuation of the Jewish people. They became living miracles when they took it upon themselves to stand up to Greek oppression. And in each generation, Jews have continued this miracle by renewing their commitment to Judaism and the Jewish people in the face of virulent physical and cultural persecution.

And for 2,200 years, God has been looking down and saying, "Yes, your miracle is greater than Mine."

Chanukah is the time when we should be declaring: Ask not what the Jewish people can do for you, but rather what you can do for the Jewish people.

Chanukah summons us to dedicate our time and effort to the Jewish people.

Chanukah is the time for us to become a miracle.

Tu B'Shvat

Are You the Cat in the Cradle?

If you stand by a tree and continuously watch it grow,
you will not see anything. But if you nourish it
at every moment, prune the branches
and protect it from harm, it will grow in its right time
(Reb Uri of Strelisk)

*E*VENTUALLY, our house quiets down.

Today was especially busy because tomorrow is Tu B'Shvat, the New Year of the Trees. We had to organize all the fruits and help the children practice their parts in the Tu B'Shvat festivities.

But now the floor is clean (all the squished figs have been scraped off); the dishes and homework are done. The kids are bathed, teeth brushed, stories read and they're finally in bed. During the day, this quiet is what a parent yearns for and I would enjoy it now if I weren't so exhausted. I decide not to fight my exhaustion but to embrace it.

I slip into the boys' room, sit down on the floor, and watch our eight and twelve-year-old sons as they lie there, asleep. They are so peaceful, their stillness in such contrast to their high energy levels during the day.

I watch them and a spiritual awakening occurs. Maybe it's just my own wishful thinking, or maybe it's all this Tu B'Shvat nature talk, but suddenly I imagine that if I sit here beside them long enough, I will actually be able to see them grow.

There are moments which you can point to and say, "Here's growth," like a baby eating her first foods, taking her first steps, speaking her first words. But usually the magic and beauty of raising children is in the *process*. Tu B'Shvat and children go hand in hand because they are both about celebrating the *process* of growth.

The Bible tells us: "A person is a tree of the field" (Deuteronomy 20:19).

Reb Uri of Strelisk explained the parallel this way:

If you stand by a tree and continuously watch it grow, you will not see anything. But if you nourish it at every moment, prune the branches and protect it from harm, it will grow in its right time. So it is with a person. A person only needs proper nourishment, and the strength to overcome that which hinders him, in order to flourish and reach his height. But it is not appropriate to check every hour how much he has grown (*Imrei Kodesh*).

We celebrate the first steps, the first words, the first day at school, but on Tu B'Shvat, it is the uneventful process which we celebrate.

I, like many, belong to the "Cat's in the Cradle" generation (words and music by Harry Chapin and Sandy Chapin):

And the cat's in the cradle and the silver spoon, Little boy blue and the man in the moon. "When you coming home, Dad?" "I don't know when, But we'll get together then, Son. You know we'll have a good time then."

Well, not me. I want to be there. I want to be there during all the moments when you don't see any growing going on, but it's happening just the same.

All I want is to sit back and be part of the process. That is the celebration of children, and the cause for joy on Tu B'Shvat. For Tu B'Shvat is the day we thank God for letting us be part of this miraculous, natural world.

You are Someone's Dream

*No matter how involved we get in our reality,
we should never forget our dreams*

Our son Avi is a year away from his *bar mitzvah*. He is getting tall and filling out a little bit. He wears my socks and some of my T-shirts. He is becoming something he wasn't before. He was a child before and now...well, I'm not quite sure.

As parents, you spend a lot of time waiting for your children to do things. You wait for them to smile, to walk, talk and toilet-train. To share, to read, to ride a bike, to recite the *Shema*, to sit through a prayer service, to be successful in school, to mature, to become responsible.

It's a lot of waiting.

What are we waiting for? We're waiting for our dream. That is what children are. They are their parents' dream: Two dreamt about creating a third. It is so amazing to think that I was someone else's dream – a dream that became a reality.

This is what we celebrate on Tu B'Shvat. On this holiday we recognize the process the seed went through. The seed needs so much strength, tenacity and patience to wait for the day it will break through the ground, to finally be able to receive its nourishment from the rays of the sun and its vitality from the air.

The seed needs to wait in hope of becoming a seedling, then a stock, then a trunk, then a branch and a leaf, and finally a fruit. For such a long time, the seed dreamt of the fruit, and now, finally, the seed is so proud.

Tu B'Shvat is the night we turn to our children and say to them: "Do you know what you are? You are a seed; you are a dream." And we beg them, "Never forget what you are."

This idea is given expression in the choice of wine we drink during the Tu B'Shvat *seder*.

We drink four cups, just like on Passover:

The first is filled with white wine.
The second is white with a little red.
The third is half-white, half-red.
And the last is red with a little white.

Here, too, we have the message of a dream becoming a reality.

The clear white wine represents the world of dreams, while the red symbolizes the flesh-and-blood reality.

We begin with white wine – the dream, the seed, the baby. And we progress, watching the dream actualize itself.

The last cup holds the sweetest message, because instead of it paralleling the first cup and being totally red, it is red wine with just a hint of white. Why?

Because no matter how involved we get in our reality, we should never forget our dreams. We should never forget our roots, the seed from which we sprang.

We should never forget what we really are: a lofty dream full of possibility.

Purim

Drinking for Clarity

*There is a deeper level to our reality
that cannot possibly be perceived when sober*

*A*s PURIM DRAWS CLOSER, we owe it an apology. Usually this holiday is treated as a Jewish Mardi Gras – a Jewish Halloween with costumes and treats (though no tricks). However, our Purim activities are trying to teach us profound messages for life. It's time to stop and ponder the spiritual awakenings offered by such Purim activities as reading the Scroll of Esther and getting stone drunk on Purim day.

There is a humorous tale which illustrates one of Purim's most important messages:

During the Stalinist regime, a poor farmer is exiled to Siberia on charges of espionage. In the middle of winter, his wife writes him a letter: "I have to plow our field to plant the potato crop, but the ox has died. What shall I do?"

Her husband writes back, "DON'T PLOW THAT FIELD! I've buried an entire cache of rifles and hand-grenades there."

Several days later, a truckload of Russian soldiers descends upon the farm and they furiously begin to dig for the guns, but find nothing. Hours later, with nothing to show for their efforts, they return to their truck and drive off. The farmer's distraught wife writes to her husband, "The Russians were here, and they turned the entire field over from beginning to end." The farmer writes back, "NOW you can plant the potatoes."

What makes this so funny?

We think we know where the story is headed, and then suddenly it hits us with a boomerang punch line that overthrows all our previous notions. (The story and its development were contributed by Rabbi Eliezer Shore.)

This is also true regarding the story in the Scroll of Esther.

The Jewish nation is put in peril when Haman, a high royal minister, decrees that everyone must bow down to him. He meets Mordechai on the street, and Mordechai refuses to bow. Haman becomes infuriated and decides to build a gallow for Mordechai, and for good measure secures from the king the right to have all the Jews slaughtered on the thirteenth of Adar, the day which will later become the holiday of Purim.

But who ends up being hanged on the gallows? Haman, himself!

And the thirteenth of Adar turns from being a day of national slaughter to a holiday remembered throughout Jewish history.

What is the message?

We read of the Russian soldiers digging up a poor woman's land, only to find out that they were actually doing her plowing for her and ensuring her livelihood for the coming year. And we read of the gallows of hatred being raised for a Jew, only to find hatred being hanged on those same gallows.

The word Purim means lots, as in a lottery. Purim is a day when we look at all the events in our lives that seem to occur as randomly as someone picking a lottery ticket from a barrel, and realize that everything was meant to be. It is the day when we see that all the seemingly meaningless and painful events in our life are, in actuality, preparing our fields for a new potato crop. The Scroll of Esther teaches that good will ultimately come even from the bad.

Now it becomes clear why the Sages instruct us to drink on Purim.

They teach: "A person is obligated to drink until he doesn't know the difference between 'Cursed is Haman' and 'Blessed is Mordechai.'"

Rationally, it is very hard to conceive of pain being beneficial. That's why we drink: to be able to bypass our rational mind. Drinking on Purim does not make us confused; rather, it gives us a deeper clarity as to how reality functions. It is this clarity which allows us a good laugh at those Russian soldiers, doing their damnedest to harm the poor peasants.

We can look at all of Jewish history with "Purim eyes."

With "Purim eyes," we must thank the six Arab nations who attacked the newly-founded State of Israel in 1948, trying to drive them into the sea. Their hostility actually allowed the Israelis to increase their borders to an extent which would have been impossible by treaty or international agreement.

With "Purim eyes" we must thank Jordan's King Hussein for shelling East Jerusalem during the Six Day War. His attack gave Israel the opportunity to reunify East and West Jerusalem.

With historic perspective, we can sometimes understand how the seemingly evil actually had a beneficial purpose. On Purim, we celebrate this perspective and try to apply it to the here-and-now. The fundamental Jewish belief that things will work out for the best is not based on wishful thinking. Instead, it is a profound awakening to the fact that everything is orchestrated from above with purpose and meaning.

Indeed, everything that happens is for the good. You may just need a good stiff drink to be able to see it!

Lechaim! Happy Purim!

Purim Spirituality

A holy drunkard sees only One, and nothing else
(Rabbi Shlomo Carlebach)

SMASHED, INTOXICATED, SLOSHED, feeling-no-pain and drunk-as-a-skunk are some of the states that can describe us on Purim. This is the holiday when Jews are commanded to drink. However, nowhere in Jewish tradition does it actually say that one should get drunk on Purim. What it does say, literally, is: "One should become *perfumed* on Purim," which is understood as referring to drink. The *Me'iri* explains that this wording is very precise. By saying, "One should become perfumed," the Sages were clarifying the type of drinking we should be doing. If you can get drunk and still smell nice, like perfume (i.e., act in a pleasant fashion), then by all means go ahead. But if, after a few shots, you start getting obnoxious and using foul language, then you have no right to get drunk on Purim.

Our Sages taught us that when wine goes in, secrets come out. As we drink on Purim our innermost selves are revealed. If you think that in your very core you're obnoxious and foul, then please don't drink. But if it is clear to you that the innermost part of you is pure and sweet, then go ahead and drink your Purim wine. This will only enhance your journey and help you reach that most hidden place. In Judaism we believe that the core of a person is totally whole, pure and perfect. Yet, as we live our lives on this earth, we are not always able to connect to that place.

Rabbi Shlomo Carlebach talked about two kinds of drunks: the "drunk" drunk and the "holy" drunk.

He asked: "What's the difference between drunk drunk and holy drunk? A non-holy drunkard, if he sees ten people, he sees a hundred; if he sees a million, he might say he sees ten million. A holy drunkard sees only One, and nothing else."

Rabbi Carlebach was teaching us that drinking in a "perfumed" way helps us reach a state where all the barriers we have erected between our conscious selves and our innermost selves, and all the barriers we have erected between ourselves and others simply fall away.

On Purim, I tried to keep that idea in my mind as the wine, vodka, scotch and bourbon "perfumed" me. I came up with the following conclusions:

- When we're sober there are some people we like and some people we don't like, but when we're "holy drunk," we love everyone.
- When we're sober, sometimes we caress our children and other times we yell at them, but when we're "holy drunk," we only want to kiss our children a million times over.
- When we're sober, we have good things to say and bad things to say, but when we're "holy drunk," there is only good.
- When we're sober, we think twenty times before going over to someone's house, but when we're "holy drunk" it's so easy to knock on that door.

Rabbi Shlomo Carlebach was so connected to his core that he knew how to be a Purim Jew all year long. He showed us how to go beyond our self-imposed limitations and the artificial barriers we erect.

Every year, sobering up is a painful process. I get a terrible stomachache and feel so tired. Yet the physical hangover is nothing compared to the emotional and spiritual angst of losing my Purim consciousness.

We need so much strength to stop ourselves from yelling at our children. We need so much strength to see the good in each person.

May we never lose this awareness. May we keep our Purim high, our Purim awakenings, all year long.

Sadness, Light and Meaning

They had light because they had meaning

ISN'T ANYONE HAPPY anymore? I mean *really* happy. The answer, of course, is yes. There are millions of families who sit together around the dinner table every night, people who have good friends, good times and fulfilling work.

However, more and more, when we meet someone who's always smiling and happy, we kind of think they're not for real. We've grown so cynical, it's almost as if we've become experts in bitterness and sadness.

What creates sadness?

One type of sadness is caused by emotional or physical pain. But then there is a sadness that is caused by a way of thinking, not connected to any specific painful occurrence.

Both Reb Levi Yitzhak of Berditchev and logotherapist Viktor Frankl maintained that people can deal with almost any "what" if they have a good enough "why." They can bear a lot of pain and discomfort if they know there is a purpose for it. Athletes and musicians endure pain while training. Chemotherapy patients are willing to go through extreme nausea and discomfort because they hope the treatment will save their lives. Pain does not necessarily create sadness. And relief from pain does not necessarily make the sadness go away. However, sadness can be overcome by finding meaning in our everyday lives.

This explains the climax of the Purim story. After Haman is hanged and the Jews are triumphant over their enemies, the Scroll of Esther says (8:16): "And the Jews had light, happiness, joy and honor."

What was the cause of their joy?

Undoubtedly, it was because the gallows raised for Mordechai were used for Haman, and Purim day, the day chosen by Haman as the day of Jewish slaughter, was turned into a day of victory, as the Jews received permission to arm themselves and fight back against their attackers.

But I think there was an additional reason for their happiness. We are told that in addition to happiness, joy and honor, "the Jews had light." What is the significance of this "light"? Aren't happiness, joy and honor enough?

Happiness, joy and honor can fully be experienced as a result of the end of sadness. As the oppressive forces were lifted, the Jews' sadness was replaced with happiness.

Light is different. In Judaism, light is related to wisdom and understanding. The Jews had light because they *understood* that all the troubles they had gone through – all the anguish they endured – had meaning. The Jews had light because they understood why Esther, a Jewish woman, had to defile herself for the Persian king; why Mordechai's deed of saving the king initially went unnoticed; why Haman had to rise to power and control the king's court and the land as a whole.

They had light because they had meaning.

Rabbi Yitzchak Hutner, a leading twentieth-century Jewish scholar, expressed this idea with the following parable:

> The guards of a city were instructed to learn how to recognize people at night. The first guard was given a candle. The second guard felt discriminated against because he did not get a candle. At the beginning, the first guard was understandably much more successful at his job. But ultimately, the second guard became a much better scout. Why? Because the second guard had to learn

to see even when there was no light. He had to learn to find and use the slightest glimmer of light in the darkness. So, in the end, which of the guards had more light?

In Judaism, the belief that we live in an ethically structured universe allows us to find meaning in a world full of pain. In Judaism, we believe that woven into the fabric of reality is the ethical clause. This clause obligates personal and universal accountability.

God is the ethical clause. Only God has the infinitely broad view to make sure all rights are rewarded and all evils corrected.

In Judaism, when we say we believe in God, we're really saying that there's meaning to everything that happens to us, no matter how painful.

This is what the Jews of Shushan understood. They had light because they saw their here-and-now as having meaning, as being directed by forces greater than themselves.

In Judaism, we believe in an historic, directing force, greater than ourselves, which gives meaning to all aspects of life, both the good and the bad. In mystical language, we notice that the Hebrew word for pain, *tza'ar*, and the Hebrew word for youth, *tza'ir*, share the same three-letter root (*Tzadi, Ayin, Resh*). What helps translate pain into youth is the one added letter in the word *tza'ir*, the letter *Yud*. The letter *Yud* symbolizes God's name. This wordplay says it all. Pain without God equals pain without meaning, as in the Hebrew word *tza'ar* – pain, a word without the letter *Yud*. Here, pain is just plain pain. The Hebrew word *tza'ir*, with a *Yud*, means to be youthful and energetic, to be ready to take on the pain of life because it, too, has meaning.

Passover

Becoming a Chisel:
The Shift from Purim to Passover

When I have become a chisel,
then I am truly free to sculpt my path through life

*E*IGHT YEARS AGO, I found myself on an overnight hike in the desert with 70 junior high school students. The first day ended with a strenuous mountain climb. We reached the peak just as the sun was setting and enjoyed a breathtaking view of the desert valley. As group leader, I wanted to give voice to the spiritual feeling of the moment, so I borrowed a guitar, stood in front of the kids and prepared to teach them a song. Before I began, I whispered a little prayer: Dear God, You and I know that I never learned how to play the guitar. But You and I also know how much I want to make this moment special for the children. So I'll move my hands, God, and, please, YOU make the music!

With that prayer in my heart, I began strumming and singing, until one of the teachers came over and said in my ear, "Just sing. The guitar sounds terrible."

You might say that God did not answer my prayer. But after my initial disappointment, I realized that there *had* been an answer, loud and clear. The answer was "NO." And this answer told me more. It said: "Do your homework! Train your fingers and your mind so you'll be able to play the guitar yourself."

God is much more of an educator than a miracle worker. Or you could say that the greatest miracle worker is the one that helps the other become a source of miracles.

My first "guitar experience" raised a crucial question about freedom: At that moment, did I truly have the freedom to play the guitar? The answer is complex, and awakens us to the two types of freedom we experience during this holiday season: Purim freedom and Passover freedom.

Purim freedom comes from letting it all hang out. On Purim, we drink in order to break down the barriers between people. We want to free ourselves from all the limitations we have imposed upon ourselves and others.

On the Purim level, I definitely had the freedom to play the guitar.

But Passover freedom is exactly the opposite. Passover freedom comes from learning how to control and train ourselves. A guitar string may want to hang loose, but it will only sound good if it's finely tuned. On the Passover level, I definitely did *not* have the freedom to play the guitar at that moment.

Moses attempted to educate Pharaoh and the Jewish people about Passover freedom when he repeatedly said to Pharaoh, "Let My people go." That, however, is not the full biblical sentence. The full sentence is, "Moses said to Pharaoh, 'So says God: Let My people go *so they shall serve Me.*'"

Moses was talking about freedom, but not freedom for its own sake. Rather, it was the freedom to serve God and live according to the greatest ethical code of all time, the freedom to master, through daily practice, a lofty, enlightened code of behavior. The Jewish people needed to be free in order to train themselves to be a Godly people.

Passover teaches that I only became free to play the guitar seven years after that hike, when I started taking guitar lessons.

Passover teaches that we are only free to be moral human beings when we learn how. This does not negate our deep, intuitive ethical sense. It is simply the meaning of true freedom.

We attain freedom from our desires when we learn how to master them and channel them positively. Channeling one's desires does not come from letting them all hang out, but from daily self-restraint and dedication to a spiritual lifestyle. This is Passover freedom.

The Hebrew word for freedom is *cherut*. This is closely related to the word *charut* – "engraved." Engraved means permanent, not changeable. Yet freedom seems to imply the ability to choose and change! How can the same letters spell out two seemingly opposite concepts? We see that true freedom comes from the ability to bring into reality that which has already been "engraved" in us as potential.

Judaism believes that we are born with an intuitive moral sense. Yet, in this complex world, we are not always sure which among many confusing options is the correct choice.

Is it ethical to copy audio or video tapes? What are the ethical consequences if I do not pick up fallen shards of glass and the person behind me is injured by them? Such dilemmas are daily occurrences for the ethically sensitive.

Freedom through self-training is also the key to dealing with our emotions.

I become emotionally free when I've learned to control my emotions and not let them control me. It is only when I have learned how to engrave the proper actions upon myself that I am truly free. When I have become a chisel, then I am truly free to sculpt my path through life.

Moses, 3,000 years ago, knew that I would not be able to play the guitar that day in the desert. For I had not yet engraved that skill upon my heart and upon my hands. I was not yet free.

The Broken Matzah

As long as all people are not free, we are still a little broken

$\mathcal{M}$Y PARENTS never told me to care about Jews in other parts of the world. They didn't have to, because at our *seder* there was a special plate for the "*Matzah* of Hope," the *matzah* we did not eat, the *matzah* we were saving for all the Soviet Jews trapped behind the Iron Curtain.

It was only later in life that I came to realize there was a ritual traditionally conducted at the *seder* which conveys the same exact message as the *matzah* of hope. I am referring to *Yachatz* – the breaking of the *matzah*. For *Yachatz*, we take the symbol of freedom on the night that we celebrate our freedom, and break it in half.

Why do we break our symbol of freedom?

The chassidic master of Raminov told the following story:

In my synagogue, there were two small boys, five-years-old. They were cute and energetic and were always running up and down the aisles. Finally, I took them aside. "Shmuel and Chaim, I have an important job for you. I need two boys to come early to *shul* and hand out the prayer books and the *Chumashim* to everyone. Do you think you could do that?" They nodded happily.

From that time on they were just as energetic as ever, but they became a beautiful pair of helpers. As they grew up, I saw they needed more tasks, so I started to pay them to clean the synagogue. As I watched them grow up, I was witness to the development of an inspiring friendship. So I was deeply saddened when I overheard them talking about their impending separation:

"Shmuel, tomorrow is the day."

"I know, Chaim. What are we going to do?"

"There is nothing to do; we are just going to have to say good-bye."

"Say good-bye? You are my best friend! I wouldn't even know how," said Shmuel.

"Shmuel, tomorrow we are going off to different *yeshivahs* in different towns. But I have an idea: Later on today, after the midday prayers, we'll meet in the forest and say good-bye."

I couldn't control my curiosity. How do two such friends say good-bye? I wondered. I decided to hide in the forest and see.

From my hiding place, I watched Chaim and Shmuel approach each other. It seems they had decided to give each other photographs of themselves. Yet they did not just exchange pictures. You see, Chaim took a picture of himself, tore it in half and gave half to Shmuel. Shmuel took his picture, tore it in half and gave half to Chaim.

Do you understand what they were saying? They were saying that without each other, they weren't whole. Without each other they were only half a person.

"So, too," the Rebbe of Raminov concluded, "we break the *matzah* to remind us that as long as *all* people are not free, we are still a little broken."

How wonderful it is to break the *matzah*! How wonderful it is that on our night of freedom, we remain focused on the need for the freedom of every human being – to remind ourselves that as Jews, we were chosen to bring the message of freedom not only to the Jewish people but to the whole world.

Fifty years ago we had a *matzah* of hope for those we lost in the Holocaust.

Twenty years ago we had a *matzah* of hope for the Jews of the Soviet Union.

This year, fifty percent of the world's young Jews are being lost to apathy, ignorance and assimilation.

Today our *matzahs* are so broken.

Today the *matzah* of hope takes on new meaning.

I hope that one day soon there will be no more need to break our *matzah*.

Mezuzah: A Ticket to Freedom

It's not the doorpost which is holding up the house,
but the mezuzah which is upon it

THREE WEEKS before my wedding (summer of '86), I got lost walking back from the synagogue in Atlantic City, New Jersey. Although I was worried at first, my childhood Monopoly skills kicked in. Like most of us, the board was etched into my memory, and I knew that even though I was on Virginia St., I would be able to find my way back to Mediterranean.

Looking closely at the street signs and house numbers, I began to realize that there were no *mezuzahs* on the doors. I know I should not have been surprised, but as an Israeli, I was used to seeing a *mezuzah* on almost every door frame. It felt really strange to pass by so many houses and not see one *mezuzah*.

The *mezuzah* dates back to one of the most crucial events in Jewish history: the night of the Exodus from Egypt. The night before the Jews were to leave Egypt, God commanded them: "You shall take a bunch of hyssop and dip it in the blood and touch the doorposts...." (Exodus 12:21–23).

The ones who did so were freed, the ones who did not stayed in bondage. By requiring the painting of the doorposts, God was sending a clear message: The Jews are going to be set free, but not everyone is going to leave – only those who have the courage, the *chutzpah*, to take the blood of an animal worshiped by the Egyptians, and place that blood in a public place, will be taken out of slavery.

It was as if God was challenging every Jew to proclaim, "I am proud to be Jewish." Sadly enough, our oral tradition teaches that not all the Jews could bring themselves to place the blood outside their homes. In fact, it records that only one-fifth of the Jewish population was actually taken out of Egypt. Throughout history, Jews have repeatedly faced the dilemma of how public they should be with their Judaism.

When I visited the former Soviet Union, I had the privilege of meeting Russian-Jewish refuseniks who were put in jail because they would not take down their *mezuzah*. These people were miles away from any Jewish home, but they were never lost. I wish we had *their mezuzah* on our door.

Mezuzah comes from the Hebrew root *zuz*, which means "movement." This intrigues me. How can a box that is permanently attached to the doorpost be called "movement"? The answer lies in the historic setting of the first *mezuzah*. That night, a few hours prior to the Exodus from Egypt, a *mezuzah* meant movement: the movement from being a devout Jew on the inside, to being a devout Jew publicly; from the willingness to have a *seder* indoors in the land of Egypt, to actually painting my doorpost so that everyone will know where I stand.

Why were only a fifth of our people willing to do so? Here the oral tradition illuminates a very human side of us all: No one likes to be different. No one likes to stand out.

I believe, however, that Judaism wants us to be public and to be noticeable. As Jews, we were chosen to carry a message to the world. The Passover message is that everyone has the right to be free to follow a moral life. God expects us to stand up for this message, to actively promote and guard it.

If we look back at the Purim story, we see that Esther found the strength to reveal her hidden identity and become a messenger of the Jewish people. She discovered a wellspring of determination that allowed her to risk social banishment or death for her people. At the end, Esther revealed her most veiled secret: "I am a Jew!" and by doing so, saved all her people from destruction.

Esther's behavior teaches us a very important lesson about being Jewish in the Diaspora. Often, we have to hide our Jewishness to get ahead (and most of the time it is *not* in order to save the Jewish people).

A friend of mine worked for a New York company for twenty years. He went to synagogue every Shabbat but never wore a *kippah* to work. He was sure it would hurt his chances for promotion.

The *mezuzah* teaches us not to hide our Jewishness. The *mezuzah* teaches us to reveal our heritage, even if it means economic or social discomfort. The *mezuzah* teaches us that there will come a time when we will not be able to hide anymore.

As we leave our homes, we look to our doorposts for the inspiration that the *mezuzah* gives us. We touch the *mezuzah* and kiss it with our fingers, with the recognition that we are now moving from our private home into the public world. At home, I know I'm Jewish. I have Jewish books on my shelf, Jewish music on my stereo, Jewish symbols on my walls, Jewish clothes in my closet and Jewish food in my refrigerator. My house is my sanctuary from the outside world. The challenge of the *mezuzah* is: Will I pick up the gauntlet of public Jewish life as I move ("*zuz*") into the world?

The *mezuzah* teaches us to be the same person inside and outside our homes, and that our Judaism should be a constant in our lives – one thread which links all the events of our day. The *mezuzah* links the public street to our private home. It links our homes in America to those in Israel, and to those in Russia. It reconnects our homes to those brick-baked dwellings of our ancestors in Egypt, who had the courage to publicly proclaim their Jewishness.

Tzvi Michael pointed out that in a Jewish home, it's not the doorpost which is holding up the house, but the *mezuzah* upon it. I would add that it is the *mezuzah* and its message which is holding up and supporting the Jewish people.

A Sense of Simplicity

Chametz is symbolic of all that has risen, gotten puffed up and out of proportion in our life. Chametz is everything I really don't need, and as I rid myself of all the excess, I become more ready to partake of the symbol of freedom

BEFORE MY AMERICAN LECTURE TOUR, I took on extra work so I'd be able to buy toys for my kids. In Florida, I went to "Toys 'R Us," which, after my visit, changed its name to "Toys 'R Me." I bought hundreds of dollars' worth of toys for my kids. Hey, it was all good stuff; hockey sticks (they were a real pain to pack), a Walkman shaped like R2D2, flashlights, videos, books, mountains of Lego, board games (Othello and Sorry), a big bag of army men for Yonatan, our five-year-old, and a big soft doll for Shira Adina. The doll has red hair because that is Shira Adina's hair color. It's great buying toys for your kids and feeling like a good father! What I can't understand is why my kids are just as happy with an empty milk carton, two rocks and a stick.

The *Maharal*, a sixteenth-century Czechoslovakian rabbi, discusses this question in the context of *matzah*. *Matzah* is called "poor man's bread." In Deuteronomy 16:3, it says: "You shall eat *matzah* for seven days. This shall be poor man's bread since you left Egypt in a rush. You will then remember the day you left Egypt all the days of your life."

Matzah as "poor man's bread" is usually viewed in a negative light.

It's just flour and water, all a poor person can afford. On *seder* night it's eaten in a rush, like a slave whose time is not his own. Moreover, we break the *matzah* to identify with poor people who always save half of their food for later, never knowing where the next meal will come from.

However, the *Maharal* sees this description of *matzah* in a positive light. He agrees that *matzah* is simple, in the sense that it's just flour and water, yet he sees this simplicity as one of the main lessons of Passover.

Eating *matzah* is the climax of the removal of all the *chametz*, the leaven, from our homes. *Chametz* is symbolic of all that has risen, gotten puffed up and out of proportion in our life. *Chametz* is everything I really don't need, and as I rid myself of all the excess, I become more ready to partake of the symbol of freedom. As I recognize what is inflated in my life, I ask myself: What do I really need in order to give meaning to my existence?

This is the question that needs to be asked in order to become spiritually awakened.

How many toys do children need in order to be happy? How many do adults need? How many shirts are enough? How many CDs? Why do I need so much? Is it because I am so empty of meaningful things that I always need more meaningless things?

Matzah is simple. On Passover we are commanded to ingest simplicity because during this holiday we are trying to retrieve that simplicity. When Annette and I decided to get married, it was so simple. I said to her, "I want to be with you," and she replied "And I want you to be with me." Now, years later, the relationship is full of beautiful reasons to stay together, and other reasons which keep us apart. As I eat the *matzah*, I am also trying to become simple, trying to give new life to the awesome simplicity of our relationship. "I want to be with you," and she replied, "And I want you to be with me." So simple.

We love our children like there is no tomorrow. Can we ever have enough kisses for our children? Yet it gets so mixed up. But then at the *seder* table, it's clear to me: I love you, I don't want to hurt you anymore and I am so sorry for all my mistakes. Please, I'm begging you, let's go back to a simpler time and place.

In high school, maybe even in college, it was clear to us how we were going to make an impact on the world with our idealism. Now, we are older and wiser – or maybe not wiser, just older. The ability to be simple is also the ability to be free. If I believe in my ideals, I must act on them. Simplicity gives us the focus and the freedom to act, because we have to do what we have to do.

We live in a complex world. We have to learn to function in it, use the system and even pay homage to it. However, the *Maharal* teaches us to retain an inner sense of simplicity.

The stack of toys remains in the corner as my children build rock castles, because rock castles are so simple. And they are also free!

I Know Pain

Transforming pain into an ethical responsibility towards others

I KNOW PAIN. In fact, pain and I are old companions. In elementary
school, I experienced the pain of being held in low regard. I learned
deep loneliness at age fourteen, spending a year alone in Israel, without
family. As a troubled teenager, I knew the panic of being out of control
and the anguish of having others trying to control my life. As an Israeli
soldier I knew the sorrow of having to put people into jail cells. Dating,
I had my heart broken by women I wanted to call my own.

I like my pain. It gives me an out whenever I mess up. I can
rationalize and say: Why do I mess up? It's not because I'm a bad person;
it's because I still have unresolved pain.

This might be the pain of not being loved enough or not having
enough childhood friends, the pain of a broken relationship or whatever
pain I carry around. If we have pain, I don't think we need to go to a
psychologist, because everyone has pain. The question is what we do
with it.

If we choose unhealthy ways of dealing with our pain, such as the
inability to commit to a relationship or repetitive life failures, then we
might need a psychologist to help us choose better behaviors. However,
pain in itself is normal.

In Judaism, we believe pain is part of the human condition. As we approach Passover, we encounter the tremendous pain of slavery. My great-great-great-great- grandfather (twelfth century B.C.E.) was a slave. My people were slaves. I am a descendant of slaves.

On Passover, we are commanded to be in a place of bondage. This idea is reflected in the structure of the *Haggadah*. The Torah commands us to relate the story of Passover. Our oral tradition teaches the way to tell this story: "One should begin with the shame – the shame of slavery – and end with the praise – the praise of becoming free."

We may not want to enter that place of shame. We may not want to revisit those life episodes when we experienced suffering or humiliation. Nor do we want to remember all those people who tried to control us, people who were our own personal Pharaohs.

Yet the authors of the *Haggadah* understood that in order to become free, we must return to that place of shame, humiliation and servitude.

Why?

I think it's because our natural reaction to pain is to hide it. It's too painful to share with others or even to share with ourselves.

Yet we all know that ultimately we cannot hide that which causes us distress. Instead of dealing with it or controlling it, we let it control us. Instead of learning how to master our pain, we become slaves to it. A person who constantly gets angry is not a slave to his anger, but to the pain which generates his anger. Truly, his anger is an expression of his inability to be with his own painful feelings.

Therefore, the road to freedom begins when I realize that I am a slave to my pain. The road to freedom is when I stop hiding and begin to work through it.

I can say to myself: Yes, my friend hurt me, but I have the strength to be in that place of hurt and work through it, because I want to regain trust in my friend and in others.

Yes, my parents did not spend enough time with me, but I have the strength to visit the pain and work through it, so that I will have a better handle on dealing with my own children.

Yes, I made a terrible mistake dealing with my kids, but I have the strength to be in my own place of shame, so that I can figure out what went wrong and how to fix it.

So, although I like my pain because it gives me a way out, I am really not interested in excuses. I am only interested in facing my pain as a road to freedom.

Dr. Martin Luther King, Jr. was special, but not because he felt the pain of the blacks. Many people felt that pain. But Dr. King had the courage to face the experience head on. He was not afraid to feel the hurt of humiliation, and from that place of suffering he reached a place of strength. He was able to demand moral accountability from white Americans. But even more crucial to the success of the civil rights movement was his demand for moral accountability from the blacks. His aim was to avoid creating a society of victims, but rather to turn their pain into the opportunity to ethically elevate all people, so that such social evils would no longer be committed.

We, too, are told every year to feel the pain of the Egyptian servitude. "Every person must feel as if he himself went out of Egypt" (the Passover *Haggadah*). Yet, as we leave Egypt, the Torah directs us to learn the lesson of our national pain: "Do not hurt the feelings of a stranger or oppress him, for you were strangers in Egypt" (Exodus 22:20, 23:9; Leviticus 19:34; Deuteronomy 10:19).

The Torah does not want us to forget our pain, neither on Passover nor during the year. It wants us to be with our pain for the express purpose of transforming it into an ethical responsibility towards others who are experiencing the evils that we suffered.

This translates into a potent personal message: Do not hide from your pain. Learn to be with it and learn how to transform it into a wellspring of empathy for others. As a rabbi and counselor, I have learned that the greatest gift I can give is empathy, to listen to others' pain and be with them, not because I have such a big heart, but because I too have suffered.

I am able to say with full confidence, "I know you can climb out of your deep, dark hole, because I climbed out of mine."

Dayeinu: Becoming Free

A recognition of the importance of each and every step

$\mathcal{A}$ s A CHILD I always loved singing *Dayeinu* at the *seder*. The song had a great chorus – one word, easily mastered, with a nice ring to it, even if I didn't know what it meant. About twenty years later, I finally looked it up and was puzzled to find out that *Dayeinu* means: "It would have been enough."

This song recounts all the steps that led up to the creation of a free Jewish nation, starting with the Exodus from Egypt, and culminating in the Jewish people celebrating in their Temple in Israel. The message is that true freedom begins with the physical and ends with the spiritual. During this process, important stages are mentioned, such as the splitting of the Red Sea, the giving of the Torah and the entering into the land of Israel.

The question arises as to why we say *Dayeinu* after each stage.

Had God given us only physical freedom but not the Torah, would that have been "enough"?

Had God given us the Torah but not taken us into the Holy Land, would that have been "enough"?

What is the author of *Dayeinu* trying to teach us?

Dayeinu is all about the process of becoming free. The first lesson is that attaining freedom is a process. However, it must be a process with a clear goal. This goal is clearly stated in the song – the establishment of a Jewish spiritual center in the land of Israel.

The second lesson is appreciation. Too often, we see the process as a means to an end. In *Dayeinu* we are taught that the process *is* the end. Each step is an end in itself. Declaring, "It would have been enough," is a recognition of the importance of each and every step. A wise person once taught me that the definition of success is the pursuit of a worthy goal, not necessarily the attainment of that goal.

We do not know if we are going to be successful in life. Yet if we know where we are going, and appreciate that each turn in our lives brings us closer, then *Dayeinu* – "It will have been enough."

The Counting of the Omer: Fighting the Enemy Within

Day by day, we elevate the coarse
"barley" parts of who we are

Due to a malfunction in the transporter, Captain Kirk of the starship Enterprise was split in two. The two halves looked exactly alike, but one was sweet, compassionate and rational, while the other was animalistic, savage and impulsive.

As the plot develops, Kirk has to come to terms with the fact that the negative qualities embodied by his double actually came from inside of him. Seeing his hidden side walking around and causing mayhem on the ship brings him to say to Bones, the ship's doctor, "I must take him back – into myself. I DON'T WANT TO. He's a brutish, mindless wolf in human form. But I must. He is me. HE IS ME!"

Bones replies, "Jim, don't take it so hard. We are all part wolf, part lamb. We need both parts. It's human to be both lamb and wolf."

Bones' reply is exactly the message of the Counting of the *Omer*.

We are told to bring an *Omer* – a biblical measure of barley – as a Temple offering. This offering initiated the counting of the days between Passover and Shavuot. Shavuot is the holiday which commemorates the giving of the Torah.

The Counting of the *Omer* is the period of the days between

Passover and Shavuot. The *Omer* offering is brought the day after Passover, the day after our Exodus from Egypt, the house of our physical bondage, and the counting continues for fifty days, as we each try to exit from our own personal Egypts. Why fifty days after already having left the land of Egypt? Because it's a lot easier to leave physical bondage than to leave the slave mentality within us.

The *Omer* offering was brought to help us learn how to deal with our "slave voice," the voice which speaks out of our basest physical drives.

One approach to mastering our physical drives is to put them on a diet. You tell yourself, "Today I'm not eating any junk food," or "Today I'm not going to lose my temper." In Judaism there is room for such an approach, yet this is not the lesson of the *Omer*. The *Omer* offering was intentionally brought from barley, which was used for cattle feed. Why bring cattle feed into the Temple and sanctify it through sacrifice? It would have made much more sense to bring wheat, which is a more refined, human food source.

Yet bringing barley – coarse cattle feed – as a sacrifice is the key to learning how to deal with our physical desires. Captain Kirk's positive side does not need the spiritual elevation of Temple life. It is Captain Kirk's "*Omer*" side that needs to be elevated.

Our natural reaction to our negative characteristics is to hide them away. We do not want to bring our selfishness, pettiness, pride, anger, weakness or greed into the Temple. Yet these are the physical qualities that need uplifting. For fifty days we bring cattle feed as an offering, because we are trying to learn how to uplift the animalistic, slave aspect of our personalities. It is the coarse, unrefined part within us that most needs a spiritual awakening.

During The Counting of the *Omer*, we are learning that true mastery of our basest "*Omer*" qualities comes through connecting them to spirituality. According to one system, we use every night during this fifty-day process to work on a different part of ourselves that needs fixing. And, day by day, we elevate the coarse, "barley" parts of who we are.

Bones is right; we are both wolf and lamb. To really leave Egypt behind, we focus for fifty days on the wolf in us. After this we are ready to receive the Torah. And so, on Shavuot, the offering brought is of wheat, not barley. After fifty days of personal refinement, we have sifted through enough barley to be worthy of human food – wheat.

By the end of the episode, the transporter is fixed, and both Kirks are placed in it and reunited: an easy technological solution to a complex existential situation.

The transporter *we* use is called the Counting of the *Omer*. We strive for spiritual freedom on Shavuot by using our "fifty-step program" for internal renewal.

As Captain Kirk walks off the transporter platform, Bones asks him, "How do you feel being one again?" As we use our *"Omer* transporter" to travel the distance from Passover to Shavuot, we need to find the courage to ask ourselves, "Am I at one with my weaknesses? What do I need to do to bring light to my darkest sides?"

Lag B'Omer

Cornerstones of Nationhood

One people with one heart

THE TALMUD tells us (*Yevamot* 62b): "Rabbi Akiva had 12,000 pairs of students, and they all died during the Counting of the *Omer* because they did not treat each other with respect."

On Lag B'Omer, the thirty-third day of the Counting of the *Omer*, we celebrate the day the students stopped dying. For thirty-two days during the spring of 135 C.E., Rabbi Akiva watched his students succumb to a deadly plague. Then, on the thirty-third day after Passover, the plague lifted. The Sages teach us that on this day the students learned their lesson.

The chassidic master, the Rebbe of Sochatchov explains: "They did not treat each other with respect, because they viewed each other as separate entities" (*Shem Meshmuel* on Leviticus, p. 302). He asks: Why do the Sages tell us that the dying occurred specifically during the *Omer*, during the time when we are preparing ourselves to receive the Torah, as the Jewish people did after the Exodus from Egypt?

He answers that the Jews only received the Torah when they came together as one people – one people with one heart.

Judaism's message is not one of personal salvation, but of a common redemption. Our history is the story of a group of people striving together to make their dream into a reality. This unity is a precondition to receiving the Torah, and to be successful in any national endeavor. This is the lesson Rabbi Akiva's students learned after thirty-two days of suffering and loss.

How can we properly mark Lag B'Omer in our time? Besides the usual custom of lighting bonfires, we can think of everyone around us as part of one entity. We can give up our quarrels and grudges. Let's use this special day as an opportunity for spiritual awakening, and truly become "one people with one heart."

Shavuot

Torah/Bible Etiquette

What is the meaning of a kiss?

On the festival of Shavuot, which commemorates the historic event of the giving of the Torah, it is appropriate to reflect on some Torah/Bible etiquette:

- It is customary not to sit on the same surface as a Bible. We don't place holy books on benches or chairs. Also, when we stack up books, we always place the Bible on top of the stack, with prayer books or other Jewish texts beneath it. Of course, a Bible should never be placed on the ground or grass, etc.
- It is customary to close a Bible when we finish using it. This is a sign of respect. According to mystical tradition, if, after study, we leave our Bible open, we put ourselves in danger of forgetting everything we just learned. Torah study is not merely an intellectual exercise. In order to integrate its ideas, we must develop an attitude of deep respect.
- It is a customary to kiss a Bible when we finish studying it.

What is the meaning of a kiss? Rabbi Shlomo Carlebach taught that we kiss because we have something very deep to share, yet we have no words. A kiss is beyond words. Every morning, as I kiss my wife and children, I experience this.

Can there ever be enough words to tell a wife or husband how much we love them? How much their caring and understanding heals us? Are there enough words to tell our children how they fill us up and give us life?

These relationships touch me in a place which is beyond intellect. This is exactly why people kiss a holy book when they finish studying it. The learning was an intellectual process of analysis. However, it touched such a deep part of them that all they can do, to truly express their feeling, is to kiss the book.

There's a story I heard from Rabbi Shlomo Carlebach. Reb Naftali Zvi, the chassidic master of the town of Ropshitz, was an extremely busy person. Up at 6:00 A.M., he began his day at the *mikveh* and then went straight to morning prayers. At 7:30, he ate breakfast with his family, and then he went out to deal with his community. The mornings were spent teaching the young children, and the afternoons were filled with adult classes, judging court cases, family counseling and supervising the kosher butcher.

By evening, he was home for supper and his day ended with his own personal studying, which took place from 9:00 P.M.–2:00 A.M. every night.

One day, he was approached by his disciples. "Rebbe, you have time for every one but us. When are you going to study with us?" The Rebbe thought for a moment and replied, "The only time I have to study is at night between 9:00–2:00. You are more than welcome to join me then."

And so it was. Every night they would come and study with their Rebbe. Since the Rebbe was a master of the mystical traditions, studying with him was an ecstatic experience. The Rebbe was able to reveal the divine light in every aspect of Jewish practice. One can imagine the communal sorrow when, after many years of service, Reb Naftali Zvi of Ropshitz passed away in his sleep.

The Shabbat after the Rebbe's death, Reb Dov, who spent many nights learning with the Rebbe, ascended the *bimah*, the synagogue's platform. "There are many who have asked me what was the most important teaching I learned from our holy master," he began. "I have thought about all the years and all the wisdom, and I can truly tell you that the deepest teaching I ever received was watching the Rebbe kiss his book when he closed it at 2:00 in the morning."

May we all learn to kiss our holy books and our dear ones with such fervor.

Hearing the Music

Crying opens up the gates, but singing knocks down the walls
(Reb Nachman of Breslov)

WATCHING A SCRIBE write a Torah scroll is an intense experience. As he lifts the quill, he utters the traditional meditation said before the writing of each and every word.

"I am writing this word in order to fulfill the *mitzvah* of writing a Torah scroll!"

Each letter must be written with the full concentration of the scribe and must conform in its preciseness to all the specifications listed in Jewish Law. The *Zohar* teaches that a Torah scroll is made up of two kinds of fire: the parchment is white fire and the ink is black fire. As you watch a scribe dip his quill into the black ink, you can imagine black fire dancing out of the inkwell to form letters which hold the wisdom and depth of the Torah.

This spiritual task reaches a climax each time the scribe writes God's name. The spiritual sanctity of this name requires the scribe to immerse himself in a *mikveh* each time before he writes these four holy Hebrew letters.

The writing of a Torah scroll is not only a precise and demanding act; it is also a spiritual path upon which the scribe walks.

Who was the first scribe in Judaism? None other than Moses. What a formidable task it must have been to write the first Torah scroll! To bring down the black fire which would inspire millions, for generations to come. Our oral tradition relates that Moses wrote the first scroll, and when he was done, he had one drop of ink left over. Now, what would you do with that one drop? A drop that could have been a vessel for the greatest wisdom and now is just left over? The Sages tell us that Moses took that drop and wrote with it on his forehead.

What does this mean? Rabbi David Ebner explains that a Torah scroll is completed only when we have learned how to write the words of the Torah upon ourselves. Just as our breath can stir a fire into flames, so, too, can our personal effort make the Torah come alive for each and every one of us. It is when we learn to write its words on our forehead that the Torah becomes our own.

Moses' action may be one of the foundations for the last *mitzvah* of the Torah. *Mitzvah* number 613 is the obligation of each man and woman to become a scribe. Every single Jew has the responsibility to write his or her own Torah scroll. This is another proof that Judaism is not a spectator sport.

No one would be the same after spending more than a year holding a quill and writing down the ethical and spiritual words of the Torah.

The Sages deduced the *mitzvah* of writing a Torah scroll from the following biblical passage: "Now write for yourself this song and teach it to the Israelites…. Make them memorize it so that this song will be a witness for the Israelites…. Moses [then] finished writing the words of this Torah in a scroll" (Deuteronomy 31:19–22).

Why does the passage refer to the Torah scroll as a song? Rabbi Menachem Schraeder of Efrat explains that the writing of the Torah is not a mechanical act but an art form. Not only are the letters beautiful works of calligraphy, but even the content follows the laws of rhyme and poetic structure, which are the basis of every sonnet or song. We also know that every verse of the Torah is sung according to an ancient musical tune passed down through the ages. So many of us were turned off to the Torah because we just didn't hear its music.

Once, during a cold and windy Siberian winter, a man became

lost in the forest. His spirits rose when he spotted a large, wooden barracks in the clearing. Reaching it, he peered in through one of the frost-glazed windows. Because of the bitter wind, he could not hear what was going on, but the sight he saw shocked him. Inside the building, he saw men and woman jumping up and down. Some were standing on tables, twisting and spinning until they fell and were caught by the people standing by. "Oh, no!" he thought in despair. "I've come upon an insane asylum!" With tears in his eyes, he walked away in further search of shelter. Little did the man know that the building he had stumbled upon was a wedding hall.

Had he heard the music, he would have realized that the people were not crazy at all. They were just dancing from joy!

How many Jews look at Jewish customs and say, "That looks crazy!" Sadly for them, all they see is the actions and not the music that pours from the soul.

A song is an expression of passion. We need to find that aspect of Torah that we feel passionate about. If we have not done so, then we have not yet learned how to make the Torah into song. We have not learned how to take that last drop of ink and inscribe it on our forehead.

On Shavuot, we should reexamine our fervor for our heritage. Some people feel there are walls between them and their Judaism. Song, passion and personal involvement can bring down the obstacles between myself and my heritage. As Reb Nachman of Breslov says: "Crying opens up the gates, but singing knocks down the walls."

Ruth: a Woman in Motion

Where you go, I shall go…

(Ruth 1:16)

*T*HE BOOK OF Ruth is a story about a woman in motion. Ruth is about to make enormous changes in her life. She is about to leave her country, her people, her culture and her religion. At that dramatic moment on a dusty and lonely road, after Orpah kisses her mother-in-law farewell, we are told that, "Ruth clung to Naomi." These few words sum up Ruth's relationship with the widowed mother of her deceased husband.

Ruth has found a kindred spirit in her mother-in-law. Ruth says, "For wherever you go, I shall go; where you lodge, I shall lodge; your nation is my nation; your God is my God. Where you die, I shall die…." (Ruth 1:16–17). With these words, she expresses her total devotion to Naomi.

These statements show the depth of Ruth's commitment to Naomi, which is the catalyst for her decision to travel with Naomi to her homeland and leave all she has ever known behind.

Ruth's willingness to change is based on ten years of observing Naomi in action. She has acquired a personal and intimate knowledge of this great woman. Therefore her decision to go with Naomi is not a frivolous one. Their relationship has developed to the degree that a

175

deep trust has been forged between them, a trust so deep that it allows Ruth to leave the familiar for the foreign.

The Sages chose Ruth as the hero of Shavuot because on this day of the Giving of the Torah, they want us to emulate her. Just as she was willing to change, so must we be ready to change. To be true to Ruth's example, we must carefully study her pattern of growth.

Ruth's major life changes are a result of a long process of observation. She has seen Naomi's successes and failures in applying her Jewish ideals to her everyday life. We should never do things blindly; the trick is to change through observation. As simple as this sounds, it is very good advice.

At times we come in contact with an inspirational spiritual idea, an idea we try to incorporate into our lives. However, Ruth teaches us that first we must ask ourselves:

- Does this idea ring true?
- Does the teacher, herself, put this idea into practice outside of the classroom?

Judaism is a religion of constant study. Through learning, we are exposed to many ideas. On the night of Shavuot, which we celebrate with an all-night learn-a-thon, Ruth is teaching us that integrating new concepts should be a slow process. We must test them to see if they really hold up in everyday life.

Now, Ruth's order of changes becomes much more understandable.

Her initial step is based on a personal connection: "Where you go, I shall go." The trust developed by this personal bond leads Ruth to also put her trust in Naomi's people: "Your people shall be my people." Only at the end of this process is Ruth willing to take on a new spiritual identity: "Your God [is] my God."

This theme of a personal connection facilitating spiritual change manifests itself in Ruth's relationship with Boaz. Ruth is a stranger in a strange land. Although she has done all she can to fit in, she is still considered an outsider. She wants to be monotheistic, but her new neighbors do not allow her to shed her past. In their eyes she is still a Moabite.

It is Boaz who sees beyond her past and recognizes how far she has come. As he learns more about her, he decides to marry her.

Ruth is a Moabite, a descendant of the nation of Moab, which means "from father." The original Moab was the product of an incestuous relationship between Lot and his daughter, directly following the destruction of Sodom. Everyone knew of Ruth's heritage, and yet the Torah tells us that Ruth became the great-grandmother of King David, from whom the Messiah is descended. This teaches that even if you come from a broken family, even if you are the product of an incestuous relationship, you can move forward and become the start of a whole new spiritual dynasty.

On Shavuot, the Sages chose to direct our attention towards a stranger. You might have thought of this holiday as the most ethnocentric of all our festivals: God gives His Divine teaching, the holy Torah, to the Jewish people alone. Yet, by reading the Book of Ruth aloud in the synagogue, we proclaim Shavuot as the holiday of learning to welcome strangers.

The giving of the Torah transformed the Jewish people into a group with a unique lifestyle, a group centered around a specific set of ideas and actions. Groups are usually formed in order to define who belongs and who doesn't. By reading the Book of Ruth on Shavuot, we learn that our "group" was formed in order to welcome all those who wish to join us in our journey of spiritual awakening.

About the Author

$\mathcal{Y}$EHOSHUA Rubin earned a master's degree in Educational Counseling from Northeastern University. Yehoshua received rabbinical ordination from Rabbi Shlomo Riskin, and was a student of Reb Shlomo Carlebach. He teaches both in high school and college, is a guidance counselor, storyteller, tour guide, writer, and the lead vocalist of his band, "The Age of Friends." Yehoshua lives in Israel with his wife Annette and their four children.

You may email Yehoshua Rubin at Rubin@UrimPublications.com.

The Holistic Haggadah
or How Will *You* be Different This Passover Night?
by Michael Kagan (forthcoming)

Besides the ritual question: "How is this night different from all other nights?" the most common questions asked during the Seder night are probably: "When's the food coming?" and "How's the kneidilech (matzah balls)?" The Holistic Judaism Haggadah asks a different type of question: "How are *you* going to be different this night? How are *you* prepared to let this night change *you*?"
The Holistic Judaism Haggadah views the evening as a very beautifully constructed experiential journey that takes us down into our own self-imposed narrowness (*Mitzraim*) and then offers us a way out into True Freedom.

hardcover, ISBN 965-7108-49-7

To find out more about our new releases,
and other works, visit our website
www.UrimPublications.com

Through our website,
register for our email list of new releases
and request a complimentary catalog.